KASHMIRI-ENGLISH DICTIONARY
FOR SECOND LANGUAGE LEARNERS

CENTRAL INSTITUTE OF INDIAN LANGUAGES
PUBLICATION NO.458

Major Indian Language: Kashmiri

KASHMIRI-ENGLISH DICTIONARY

FOR SECOND LANGUAGE LEARNERS

OMKAR N. KOUL
S. N. RAINA
ROOP KRISHEN BHAT

CENTRAL INSTITUTE OF INDIAN LANGUAGES
MANASAGANGOTRI, MYSORE, INDIA

Kashmiri-English Dictionary for Second Language Learners
Omkar N. Koul
S.N. Raina
Roop Krishen Bhat

First published: *April 2000* / *Chaitra 1922*

Address for correspondence:
Director
Central Institute of Indian Languages
Manasagangotri
MYSORE 570 006, INDIA.

Phone: 91-821-515558, 515820
Telex: 0846-268 CIIL IN
E.mail: ciil@giasbg01.vsnl.net.in
Grams: BHARATI
Fax: 0091-821-515032
Website: http://www.ciil.org

ISBN-81-7342-064-5

PRICE

Published by Dr. Omkar N. Koul, Director for
Central Institute of Indian Languages, Mysore.
Printed by Mr. S.B.Biswas, Manager, at
CIIL Printing Press, Manasagangotri, Vinoba Road,
Mysore 570 006, India.
Production: K. Srinivasacharya
Cover Design: Manohar

FOREWORD

The Central Institute of Indian Languages was established on 17th July 1969 to help, evolve and implement the language policy of the Government of India and to coordinate the development of Indian languages through research, training, material production for their use in education, administration and other public domains. The Institute has seven Regional Language Centres to impart 10 months intensive training in modern Indian languages to the teachers deputed by various State Governments and Union Territories.

The materials which are produced in the Regional Language Centres are specialized in nature as they are designed and produced to suit the need of the second language learners.

The present Dictionary was initially prepared as a Kaishmiri-English Glossary in 1976 for the use of teacher trainees who learn Kashmiri at the Northern Regional Language Centre, Patiala. As there is no other dictionary available for this purpose, it was decided to publish it in the present form. I am sure that learners of Kashmiri as a second language will find this Dictionary useful.

Omkar N. Koul
Director

KASHMIRI - ENGLISH DICTIONARY

Omkar N. Koul
S.N. Raina
Roop Krishen Bhat

INTRODUCTION

The Kashmiri-English Dictionary presents English equivalents of Kashmiri lexical items. An attempt has been made to include those lexical items which are very frequently used in both spoken and written Kashmiri. The lexical items have been compiled on the basis of their use in common speech, conversations and literary works of modern Kashmiri.

This Dictionary will be useful as a reference manual for those who are engaged in learning Kashmiri as a second or foreign language. Each entry is followed by grammatical category which may help the learner to use the item correctly. Keeping in view the difficulties a non-native speaker might face in understanding the meanings of cultural bound terms, such terms have been explained in simple words. The limitations of the present work did not allow us to furnish details of the usage of idioms and phrases associated with certain lexical items. The aim of the preparation of this Dictionary is to help the learners of Kashmiri in familiarizing themselves with the English equivalents of the Kashmiri lexical items in as simple words as possible. The usage of some of the lexical items is understood in particular context only. It has not been possible for us to present illustrations of such terms in the present Dictionary.

A Note on transliteration

We have used Roman transliteration of Kashmiri lexical items in the present Dictionary. Following is the inventory of phonemes in Kashmiri :

Vowels :

	Front	**Central**	**Back**
High	i/i	i/i:	u/u:
Mid	e/e:	A/A:	o/o:
Mid-low		a	>
Low		a:	

Consonants :

	Bi-labial	**Dental**	**Palatal**	**Rotroflex**	**Velar**	**Glottal**
Stops	p	t		T	k	
	ph	th		Th	kh	
	b	d		D	g	
Affricates		ts	c			
		tsh	ch			
			j			
Nasal	m	n				
Trill				r		
Lateral		l				
Fricatives	s	sh				h
	z					
Semi vowels	v		y			

We have followed the order of the entries in the following manner:

I	high central short vowel
I:	high central long vowel
A	high central short vowel
A:	high central long vowel
a	mid central short vowel
a:	low-central long vowel
i	high front short vowel
i:	high front long vowel
e	mid front short vowel
e:	mid front long vowel
u	high back short vowel
u:	high back long vowel
o	mid back short vowel
o:	mid back long vowel
>	mid-low back short vowel
k	unaspirated voiceless velar stop
kh	aspirated voiceless velar stop
g	unaspirated voiced velar stop
c	unaspirated voiceless palatal affricate
ch	aspirated voiceless palatal affricate
ts	unaspirated voiceless Alveolar affricate
tsh	aspirated voiceless Alveolar affricate
j	unaspirated voiced palatal affricate
z	voiced dental fricative
T	unaspirated voiceless retroflox stop
Th	aspirated voiceless retroflex stop
D	unaspirated voiced retroflex stop
t	unaspirated voiceless dental stop
th	aspirated voiceless dental stop

d	unaspirated voiced dental stop
n	voiced dental nasal
p	voiceless unaspirated bilabial stop
ph	voiceless aspirated bilabial stop
b	voiced unaspirated bilabial stop
m	voiced bilabial nasal
y	palatal frictionless continuant/semi vowel
r	trill
l	lateral
v	bilabial frictionless continuant/semi vowel
sh	palatal fricative
s	dental fricative
h	glottal fricative

List of Abbreviations

Adjective	a
Adverb	ad
Conjunction	conj
Pronoun	pr.
Feminine	f
Interjection	i
Masculine	m
Noun	n
Plural	p
Postposition	pp.
Singular	s
Verb	v
Intransitive verb	vi
causal verb	vc

Palatalization of consonants has been indicated by an apost ophe after the consonant as in the following examples : p'aTh 'on' r'ath 'month'.

Nasalization of the vowels have been indicated by the nasal sign/~/written above the vowel.

We are grateful to the Director, Central Institute of Indian Languages, Mysore for encouraging us to compile this Dictionary. We would like to thank Sh. Puran Chander De, an ex-trainee in Kashmiri, Mrs. Gopi Raina and Sh. Tej Krishen Koul for their valuable assistance rendered from time to time in compiling this Dictionary.

We are grateful to Shri R.K. Bharati for going through the manuscript and for offering valuable suggestions for its improvement.

We trust that the users will find this Dictionary useful and will offer their suggestions for its further improvement.

A

Akim (a)	اَکم	first
AgIn (m.)	اَگِن	sacred fire i.e. Agni
Ach (f.)	اَچھ	eye/eyes
Acharva:l	اَچھروال	eye lashes
Achu:t (m.)	اَچھوت	an untouchable
Ach ga:sh (m.)	اَچھ گاش	eye sight, dear one
Ach TIiTIva:ar (m.)	اَچھ ٹِٹِ وار	twinkle of an eye
Ach do:d (m.)	اَچھ دود	eye sore
Aji:b (a)	عجیب	strange
Ajdar (m.)	اَجدہر	snake/snakes, dragon
An' (f.s.)	اَنۍ	a blind woman
Anji:r kul *(m.s.)*	اَنجیرِ کُل	fig tree *Anji:r kul'* (p)
And' And' (ad)	اَندی اَندی	all round, around
Andram (m.)	اَندرم	intestines
A~z (m.)	اَنٛز	swan, goose, gander
A~zIra:vun (v.m.s.)	اَنٛزراوُن	to complete, to accomplish *A~zIra:vIn'* (m.p., f.s.) *A~zIra:vIni* (f.p.)
A~zin' (f.s.)	اَنٛزٕنۍ	swan, goose *A~zini* (p)
AD (a)	اَڈ	half *AD'* (p)
ADij (f.s.)	اَڈِج	bone *ADiji* (p)
AtI-r (f.)	عطر	perfume
Athrik'om (m.s.)	اَتھرِکیوم	moth *Athrikem'* (p)
Aphi:mci: (f)	اَفیمچی	one addict to opium
Ar (a.f.s.)	اَر	good, healthy, in good order
AlIra:vun (v.m.s.)	اَلراوُن	to move, to shake *AlIra:vIn'* (m.p.,f.s.) *AlIra:vIni* (f.p.)
Alim (m.)	عِلم	knowledge
Alish (n)	اَلِش	linseed
Arpa:vun (vt.m.s.)	اَڑپاوُن	to cause a fall
Ashik (n)	عشق	romance, love, passion
AshkIpe:ca:n (m.)	عشقِ پیچان	a flower, American Jasmine
AshTo:r (m.s.)	اَش ٹور	eye full of tears *AshTA:r'* (p)
Ashdar (m.)	اَش دَر	dragon
Ashbukh (m.)	اَش بُکھ	flow of tears
Ashba:nI (m.)	اَش بانہٕ	tear gland
As' (pr)	اَسی	we
Ahsa:s (m.)	احساس	feeling, perception

A:

A:kIl (a)	عاقل	intelligent
A:khIr (ad)	آخر	in the end, at last
A:khIri: (a)	آخری	final, last
A:jizi: (f.)	اَجزی	request, supplication

A:jizi: sa:n (ad)	عاجزی سان	humbly
A~:T (f.s.)	آنٹ	stone of a fruit
A~:T (n)	آنٹ	an inch *a~:ci* (p)
A~:TIrun (v)	آنٹرُن	to observe
A:Th (a)	آٹھ	eight
A:Th ku:nal	آٹھ کوٗنل	, octagonal
A:Th shath	آٹھ شتھ	eight hundred
A:Drun/ A:Dra:vun (v)	آڑرُن آڑراوُن	to mix, to knead *A:DIra:vun* (v.m.s.) *A:DIra:vIn'* (m.p.,f.s.) *A:DIra:vIni* (f.p.)
A~:th (a)	آنتھ	limit, vastness
A:nI (m.)	آنہٕ	looking glass, mirror
A:nakh (m.)	عانکھ	spectacles
A:phi:m (f.)	آفیم	opium
A:b (a)	عاب	a bad habit
A:bid (a)	عابد	pious, a saint, God-loving devotee
A:r (n)	آر	plum
A:rakh (m.)	عارکھ	mixture, distilled concoction
A:rakh (m.)	آرکھ	sweating, perspiration
A:l (f.s.)	آل	cardamom *A:lI* (p)
A:la:n (m.)	اعلان	announcement
A:lim (m.)	عالِم	scholar
A:lic (f.s.)	آلچ	sour cherry, damson *A:lici* (p)
A:lici kul (n)	آلچہ کُل	damson tree
A:li:sha:n (a)	عالیشان	grand
A:v'ul (a.m.s.)	آوٕل	delicate *A:vil'* (m.p.) *A:vij* (f.s.) *A:viji* (f.p.)
A:sh (n)	عاش	luxury
A:shna:v (m.)	آشناو	relative
A:shid (m.)	آشِد	Asuj -name of the sixth month (Bikrami)
A:s (m.s.)	آس	mouth
A:hi: (n)	آہی	blessings

a

akIl (f.)	عقل	wisdom, understanding
akIlmand (a)	عقلمند	wise, intelligent
akIliyath (f.)	عقلیتھ	minority
akIs (m.)	عکس	image, reflection
aki aki (ad)	اَکی اَکی	one by one
akuy (a)	اَکوے	only one/alone
akItA:ji (a)	اَکتاجی	fortyone
akItrIh (a)	اَکہ ترٕہ	thirtyone
akInamath (a)	اَکہ نمتھ	ninety one
akIvanza:h (a)	اَکہ ونزاہ	fifty one
akIvuh (a)	اَکہ وُہ	twenty one
akIshi:th (a)	اَکہ شیتھ	eighty one
akIsatath (a)	اَکہ ستتھ	seventy one

akIhA:Th (a)	اکہ ٲٹھ	sixty one
aki d>h (ad)	اکہ دۄہ	one day
aki laTi (ad)	اکہ لٹہ	once
akTar (m.)	اکٹر	actor
aktu:bar (m.)	اکتوبر	October
akli monD (a)	عقلِ مند	foolish
aksar (ad)	اکثر	often, generally
akh (a)	اکھ	one
akha:DI (m.)	اکھاڑ	field (wrestling field), arena
akhtuy (par)	اکھتُی	also
akh dama:h (ad)	اکھ دماہ	for a while
akhba:r (m.)	اخبار	newspaper/ newspapers
akh'ur/achur (m.)	اکھٕر / اچھر	letter of an alphabet
agast (m.)	اگست	August
achidA:r (f.s.)	اچھہ دار	a doll *Achida:ri* (p)
achipo:sh (n)	اچھہ پوش	a flower
atsun (v)	اژن	to enter
atshIratsh (f.s.)	اژہ رژھ	dancing girl/ prostitute, nymph *atshIratshI* (p)
ajanT (m.)	اجنٹ	agent
ajal (m.)	اجل	death
ajA:yibgar (m.)	عجائب گر	museum
az (ad)	از	today
azarvun (m.)	ازروٗن	jealousy
aza:n (a)	اَزان	ignorant, unqualified
aza:b (m.)	عذاب	discomfort, torture
aza:r (m.)	اَزار	labour pain
azkal (ad)	ازکل	nowadays, these days
azmat (f.)	عظمت	grandeur, magnificance
azta:m (ad)	ازتام	upto now, till now
az paga:h (ad)	از پگاہ	today or tomorrow
aTI (n)	اَٹہٕ	rope for the load on back
aTIba:r (m.)	اَٹہٕ بور	load on shoulders/ back
aTIhor (m.)	اَٹہٕ ہور	an ear ornament worn by Kashmiri Hindu women
aTal (a)	اٹل	final, inevitable
aTh (f.)	اَٹھ	an ear ornament worn by Kashmiri Hindu women
aTho:vuh (a)	اَٹھووہ	twenty eight
aDI (m.)	اَڈٕ	centre, a (vehicle) stand
aDIkajar (n)	اَڈٕ کجر	stuttering
aDIkAj kath (f.s.)	اَڈٕ کٲج کتھ	stuttering talk *aDIkaji kathi* (p)
aDIkol (a.m.s.)	اَڈٕ کول	one who stutters *aDIkAl'* (p) *aDIkAj* (f.s.) *aDIkaji* (p)
aDun (v)	اَڈُن	to be adament

aDImo:r (a.m.)	اَڈِمور	half dead
aDIlec (a.f.s.)	اَڈِلیچ	disabled, incomplete, weak *aDIleci* (p)
aDIl'ok (a.m.s.)	اَڈِلیوک	disabled, incomplete, weak *aDIlek'* (p)
aDIvun/ aDIvon (ad)	اَڈِوُن / اَڈِوون	a slanting place, slope
aDIvInis (ad)	اَڈِوِنِس	at a sloping place
aDIvati (ad)	اَڈِوَتِہ	on half way
aDIvarI (a)	اَڈِوَرِ	middle aged man or woman
aDun (vt.)	اَڈُن	to be adamant
atra:ph (m.)	اَطراف	loafer
atva:r (n)	اَطوار	bad deeds
athI (m.)	اَتھہٕ	hand/hands
athIpanji (m.)	اَتھہٕ پَنجہ	gloves
ath vath (f.)	اَتھہٕ وَتھ	plan, hit on a plan
athIva:s (m.)	اَتھہٕ واس	handshake, collaboration
adI kAmis (pr)	اَدِ کَمِس	whom else
adI kati (ad)	اَدِ کَتِیہ	where else
adI k'a: (ad)	اَدِ کیاہ	what else, o.k., yes
adI kar (ad)	اَدِ کَر	when?
adI kus (pr)	اَدِ کُس	who else
atIgat (m.)	اَتہٕ گَتھ	token money received by a married daughter from her parents on her visit to them for paying to her mother-in-law

adab (m.)	اَدَب	literature, good manners
adIbI sa:n (ad)	اَدبہٕ سان	with due respect
ada:vath (m.)	عداوتھ	enmity, hostility, malice
ada:ka:r (m.)	اَداکار	actor
ada:rI (m.)	اَدارِ	institute
ada:lath (f.)	عدالتھ	court
anigoT (m.s.)	اَنِگوٹ	darkness
anun (v.m.s.)	اَنُن	to bring *anIn'* (m.p.,f.s.) *anIni* (f.p.)
a~gre:z (m./f)	اَنگریز	An Englishman
a~gri:zi: (f.)	اَنگریزی	The English language
anza:n (a)	اَنزان	innocent, unaquainted
anta:karan (m.)	انتاکرن	inner thoughts, conscience
andI vandI (ad)	اَندِ وَندِ	every where, all over
andar (ad)	اَندر	inside
anda:z (m.)	اَنداز	style, imagination
ande:shi	اَندیشہ	assesment, doubt
andun (v.m.s.)	اَندُن	to accomplish *andin'* (m.p.,f.s.) *andini* (f.s.)
anpaD (a)	اَن پڑھ	illiterate
anvA:r' (f.)	اَنہٕ وارٕ	turn
anha:r (m.)	اَنہار	appearance, resemblance

apIz'o:r (m.s.)	اپزٕ ٲور	a liar *apIz'A:r'* (m.p.) *apIz'A:r* (f.s.) *apIz'a:ri* (f.p.)
apIra:d (m.)	اپراد	bad deeds, guilt, offence
apa:ri (ad)	اپارِ	across
apna:vun (v)	اپناوُن	to own
apa:ri yapo:r (ad)	اپارِ یپور	from this end to that end, across
apri:l (m.)	اپریل	April
aphIva:h (f.)	افواہ	rumour
apharvaTh (m.)	اپھروٹھ	a lie
aphta:b (m.)	افتاب	sun
aphsa:nI (m.)	افسانہ	a short story/short stories aphsar officer
aphsu:s (m.)	افسوس	alas, sorrow
aba:rath (f.)	عبارتھ	diction, a written passage
amar (m.)	امر	immortal
amal karIn' (v)	عمل کرٕنۍ	to practice, to follow
ama:poz (par)	اماپوٚز	but, in fact
ama:rI (n)	امارٕ	curiosity
ama:s	اماس	extra fat, obesity
ami ka:rnI (ad)	امہِ کارنہٕ	on this account
ami vajah kin' (ad)	امہِ وجہ کِنۍ	on this account
amun (m.)	امن	peace
amun/amno ama:n (m.)	امن و امان	peace and prosperity
amb (f.)	امب	mango *ambI* (p)
ambI A~:T (m.)	امبہٕ اَنٹ	stone of a mango
amreth (m.)	امریتھ	holy water, nectar
amru:d (m.)	امرود	guava
aya:l (m.)	عیال	family
aya:lba:r	عیال بار	having a large family
aya:sh (a)	عیاش	leading a luxurious life, voluptuous
arIz (m.)	عرض	request
arIzi: (f.)	عرضی	petition
arIvarI (m.)	ارٕ وٕرٕ	from all sides
arda:h (a)	ارداہ	eighteen
arItA:ji: (a)	ارٕتٲجی	forty eight
arItrIh (a)	ارٕترٕہ	thirty eight
arInamath (a)	ارٕنمتھ	ninety eight
arIvanza:h (a)	ارٕونزاہ	fifty eight
arIshi:th (a)	ارٕشیٖتھ	eighty eight
arIsatath (a)	ارٕستتھ	seventy eight
arIhA:Th (a)	ارٕہٲٹھ	sixty eight
argpo:sh (m.)	ارگ پوش	flowers and rice offered to God
arzi:	عرضی	petition
arzi:navi:s (m.)	عرضی نویس	petition writer
arab (a)	ارب	100 crores
arma:n (m.)	ارمان	ambition, yearning, longing
arhar (f.)	ارہر	pigeon pea

al (f.)	اَل	pumpkin *alI* (p.)
ala:kI (m.)	عَلاقہٕ	region, area
ala:y bala:y (f.)	اَلاے بَلاے	misfortune, calamity
ala:v (m.)	اَلاو	bonfire
ala:vI (par)	عَلاوٕ	besides, in addition to
alka:b (m.)	اَلقاب	honorific title
alag (m)	اَلگ	separate
alag alag (ad)	اَلگ اَلگ	separately
alIbA:n' (f.)	اَلہٕ بانٛ	plough
alImA:r' (f.s.)	اَلہٕ مآرۍ	almirah alma:ri (p)
almo:nim (m.)	اَلہٕ مونیم	aluminium
alambarda:r (m.m.)	اَلَم بَردار	head, chief, protogonist
alpa:r (m.)	اَلپار	a type of cloth
ala:h ta:la (m.)	اَللہ تعالیٰ	God, Almighty
avI (par)	اَوٕ	yes, yea
avI mkhI (par)	اَوٕ موکھہٕ	for this reason
avA:mi: mAhkham (m.)	عَوامی محکمہٕ	public office
avA:mi: ra:j (m.)	عَوامی راج	democracy
ava:m (m.)	عَوام	public
ave:za:n (v)	اَویزان	hanging
avta:r (m.)	اَوتار	incarnation
avay (ad)	اَوَے	that is why, for this reason
avar ko:Th (m.)	اَورکوٹھ	a top coat, overcoat
avza:r (m.)	اَوزار	spare parts, tools
avlay (ad)	اَولے	in initial stage
avsa:ph (m.)	اَوصاف	good qualities
ashi da:r (f.)	اَشہِ دار	stream of tears
ashob (n)	اَشوٗب	inauspicious
asIl (a)	اَصٕل	real, original
asIvun (a.m.s.)	اَسہٕ وُن	one who laughs, cheerful *asIvIn'* (m.p.m.f.s.) *asIvIni* (f.p.)
asi thi: (ad)	اَسہِ ٹھی	in our presence
asIna:vun (v.m.s.)	اَسہٕ ناوُن	to make laugh *asIna:vIn'* (m.p.,f.s.) *asIna:vIni* (f.p.)
asun (v)	اَسُن	to laugh
asta:n (m.)	اَستان	holy shrine of Muslims
asan khanga:lI (m.)	اَسن کھنگال	loud laughter
asambAli: (f.)	اَسمبلی	Legislative Assembly
asar (m.)	اَثر	influence
asma:n (m.)	اَسمان	sky
asli: (a)	اَصلی	real, original, genuine
asliyat (f.)	اَصلیت	reality
aham (a)	اَہم	important
ahamiyat (f.)	اَہمیت	importance
ahA:rI (m.)	اَہارٕ	havoc, terror
ahalka:r (m.)	اَہلکار	employee
ahmakh (ad)	اَحمق	stupid, fool

a:

a: (ad)	آ	yes, yea
a:ka:r (m.)	آکار	shape, form, structure
a:ka:sh (m.)	آکاش	sky
a:gI (m.)	آغہ	master
a:gIba:y (f.s.)	آغہ بایے	land lady, mistress
a:gur (m)	آگُر	source
a:za:d (a)	آزاد	free, independent
a:zA:di: (f.)	آزٲدی	freedom
a~:gun (m.s.)	آنگُن	compound, lawn *a~:gan* (p)
a~:car (m.)	آنچار	pickle
a:pIra:vun (vt.)	آپہ راوُن	to feed (with hand)
a:tashbA:z' (f.)	آتش بٲزۍ	fire-works
a:thva:r (f.s.)	آتھوار	Sunday
a:tshIna:vun (vt.)	آژھناوُن	to bring (a pot) in use
a:dath (m.)	عادتھ	habit
a:dam khor (m.)	آدم خور	cannibal, man eater
a:damza:d (m.)	آدم زاد	human being
a:nan pha:nan (ad)	آنن پھانن	very quickly, instantly
a:b (m.)	آب	water
a:bre:z (m.)	آبریز	urine
a:bgosh (m.)	آب گوشت	a meat dish, gravy
a:bsha:r (m.)	آبشار	waterfall, cascade
a:m (a.)	عام	common, popular

a:m (m)	آم	a threadworm
a:mto:r (ad)	عام طور	often, in general, generally
a:mdani: (f.)	آمدنی	income
a:mle:T (m.)	آملیٹ	omelette
a:yi:n (m.)	آیین	constitution
a:r (m.)	عار	mercy
a:rI (m.)	آرہ	mountain river, river bed
a:rIkAts (a.f.s.)	آرِکٕژ	helpless, pitiable *a:rIkAtsI* (f.p.) *a:rIkot* (m.s.) *a:rIkAt'* (m.p.)
a:ra:b (m.)	آراب	beginning
a:ra:dana: (f.)	آرادنا	worship, prayer
a:ra:m (m.)	آرام	relaxation, rest, comfort
a:rum (m.s.)	آرُم	one who grows vegetables *a:ram* (p)
a:rzi: (a)	عارضی	temporary
a:lutsh (m.)	آلژھ	laziness
a:lvun (v.m.s.)	آلوُن	to offer *a:lvIn'* (m.p.,f.s.) *a:lvIni* (f.p.)
a:vIra:vun (vt.m.s.)	آوراوُن	to cover, to keep busy
a:vrIn'(bal) (m.)	آورنۍ	cremation ground
a:vur (a)	آوُر	busy, pre-occupied
a:vlun (m.)	آولُن	whirlpool
a:sha: (f.)	آشا	hope

a:shakh (m.)	عاشق	lover
a:shen' (f.)	آشینی	wife *a:shni* (p)
a:shtsar (m.)	آشچر	surprise
a:shram (m.)	آشرم	hermitage, monastary
a:san vo:l (m.s.)	آسن وول	rich *a:san vA:l'* (m.p.) *a:san va:jen'* (f.s.) *a:san va:jni* (f.p.)
a:sun (v)	آسُن	to be
a:sur (m.)	آسُر	a kind of mustard seed
a:smA:n' (a)	آسمانی	sky blue colour

i

(y)inklA:b.: (a)	اِنقلاب	revolutionary
(y)intiza:m (m.)	اِنتظام	arrangement
(y)idra:r (m.)	اِدرار	urine
(y)imtiha:n (m.)	اِمتحان	examination
(y)izha:r (m.)	اِظہار	expression
(y)islA:mi: (a)	اِسلامی	of Islam, Islamic
(y)ibli:s (a)	اِبلیس	an abuse, satan
(y)ibtida: (a)	اِبتدا	beginning
(y)ira:dI (m.)	اِرادٕ	determination
(y)ilza:m (m.)	اِلزام	lame, accusation, allegation
(y)isha:rI (m.)	اِشارٕ	hint, gesture
(y)ishtiha:r (m.)	اِشتہار	poster

(y)ista:dI (a)	اِستادٕ	standing
(y)isla:h (m.)	اِصلاح	shave, reform
(y)i:d (f.)	عید	Muslim festival
(y)i:ri (v)	ایرِ	float, drift

e

(y)etiba:r	اِعتبار	belief
(y)etira:ph (m.)	اِعتراف	admission, confession
(y)ehtira:m (m.)	احترام	respect
(y)ehsa:n (m.)	احسان	obligation
(y)ehsa:s (m.)	احساس	feeling

u

ujrath (n)	اُجرتھ	wages, compensation
uta:vali: (f.)	اُتاوٕلی	haste, impatience
usta:d/vsta:d (m.)	اُستاد	artist, teacher, expert

u:

u:trI (ad)	اوٗترٕ	day before yesterday
u:r' (ad)	اوٗری	there
u:r'kun (ad)	اوٗری کُن	on that side, to that side

o

oktso:r (m.)	اوکژور	small oven with one opening

otsh (m.)	اۆژھ	slim *Atsh'* (m.p.) *Atsh* (f.s.) *atshI* (f.p.)
oD (a)	اۆڑ	half
odur (a)	اۆدُر	wet
on (a.m.s.)	اۆن	a blind man *An'* (m.p.,f.s.) *ani* (f.p.)
ongIj (f.s)	اۆنٛگٕج	finger *onglji* (p)
ongul (a)	اۆنٛگُل	finger width
op (m.)	اۆپ	flippant
obur (m.)	اۆبُر	clouds, mica
orzuv (m.)	اۆرزو	good health
osh (m.)	اۆش	tears
osu:l (m.)	اۆصوٗل	principle

o:

o:T (m.)	اوٗٹ	flour
o:l (m.)	اول	nest *A:l'* (p)
o:m (s.)	اوم	raw
o:luv (m.s.)	اولُو	potato
o:lav (p)	اولٕو	potatoes
o:s (m.s)	اوس	was

k

kIch (m.)	کٕچھ	morel
kIj (f.s.)	کٕج	a small stick, twig *kIji* (p)
kITI (a)	کٕٹ	inexperienced
kITh (a)	کٕٹھ	criticism, fault
kItI kItI (m.)	کِتہٕ کِتہٕ	tickling
kItsIna:vun (vt.)	کِژناوُن	to moist
kInIkh (m.)	کٕنٕکھ	wheat
kIn (m.)	کِن	foundation
kInun (v.m.s.)	کِنُن	to sell *kInIn'* (m.p.,f.s.) *kInIni* (f.p.)
kInIna:vun (vc.m.s.)	کِنہٕناوُن	to make sell *kInIna:vin'* (m.p.,f.s.) *kInIna:vIni* (f.p.)
kIlI (m.)	قلعہٕ	fort
kIlath (f.)	قِلتھ	scarcity
kIsI (m.)	قِصہٕ	story, gossip
kI:math (m.)	قیٖمتھ	price
kI:r (f.s.)	کیٖر	bad tempered, harsh *kI:ri* (p)
kAchvI/kachvI (m.)	کٔچھوٕ	tortoise
kAlIra:vun (vc.)	کٔلہٕراوُن	to silence someone
kAts (ad)	کٔژ	how many
kAtsh kho:r (m.s.)	کٔژھ کھور	wicker frame of a firepot *kAtsh khA:r'* (p)
kAj (f.s.)	کٔج	dumb *kaji* (p)

kAT (f.s.)	کٔٹ	girl, wench *kaci* (p)
kAtij (f.s.)	کٔتِج	a local bird, swallow *kAtiji* (p)
kAn' (f.s.)	کٔنۍ	stone *kani* (p)
kAnD' thAr (f.s.)	کٔنڈِ ٹھٔر	thorn bush *kAnD' thari* (p)
kAnD (f.s.)	کٔنڈ	crest *kanji* (p)
kAnD' ta:r (f.)	کٔنڈِ تار	barbed wire
kAnD' doph (m.)	کٔنڈِ دوپھ	thorn bush, thorn broom
kAnD' po:sh (m.)	کٔنڈِ پوش	thistle
kAmi:z (f.s.)	قمیٖض	shirt *kAmi:zI* (p)
kAm' ta:m (pr)	کٔمۍ تام	some one
kAr (f.s.)	کٔر	big piece of wood *kari* (p)
kAr (f.s.)	کٔر	(a cow) which has not given birth to a calf
kAr (f.s.)	کٔر	a log of wood *kari* (p)
kArphiv (m.)	کٔرفیو	curfew
kAliyi (m.)	کٔلیِہ	a mutton/ vegetable dish
kAshi:r (f.)	کٔشیٖر	Kashmir
kA:shir zaba:n (f.)	کٲشِر زبان	Kashmiri language
kAstu:r (m.)	کٔستوٗر	a kind of bird, thrush

[illegible]shish (f.)	کٔشِش	attraction
kAhAt (m.)	قحط	famine
kAhvAT (m.)	کٔسوٹ	touchstone
kA:k' (m.)	کاکۍ	cunning, snob
kA:ts (f.s.)	کاژ	big seissors *ka:tsI* (p)
kA:Th' (f.)	کاٹھۍ	underwear *ka:Thi* (p)
kA:tib (m.)	کاتِب	scribe
kA:d (m.)	قاد	jail
kA:n' (f.s.)	کانۍ	one eyed woman
kA~:pun (vi.)	کانپُن	to tremble, to shiver
kA:phi (a)	کافی	enough, much
kA:phir (m.)	کافِر	infidel
kA~:ph (m.)	کانپھ	fear, terror
kA:bil (a)	قابِل	able
kA:biliyath (f.)	قابلیت	efficiency
kA:m (f.)	کام	work *ka:mi* (p)
kA:mil (a)	کامِل	of high standard, completge
kA:yim (v)	قایِم	established, firm
kA:yir (a)	کایِر	lazy, craven
kA:ydI (m.)	قایدٕ	rule, primer
kA:r (f.)	کار	neck
kA:l' k'ath (ad)	کالِ کیتھ	day after tomorrow
kA:li: (f.)	کالی	Goddess of death
kA:li:nI (m.s.)	قالیٖن	carpet

kA:sh (f.s.)	کٲش	a slice of fruit *ka:shi* (p)
kA:shur (a.m.s.)	کٲشُر	Kashmiri *kA:shir'* (m.p.) *kA:shir* (f.s.) *kA:shiri* (f.p.)
kA:shir al (f.)	کٲشِر اَل	pumpkin *kA:shri alI* (p)
kA~:sIkoT (m.s.)	کانٛسہٕ کوٹ	youngest one *kA~:sIkAT'* (m.p.) *kA~:sIkAT* (f.s.) *kA~:sIkaci* (f.p.)
kA:sid (m.)	قاصِد	messenger
kA:sib (m.)	قاصِب	artist
ka~guv (m.)	کنگوو	comb *ka~gIv'* (p)
kach (m.)	کچھ	wild vegetation, grass
katsh (m.)	کَژھ	armpits
katshkar (m.)	کَژھ کر	bangles
kaza: (m.)	قضا	death
kazul (m.)	کٔزل	collorium, soot, lamp-black
kaTar (a)	کٹر	strict, bigoted
kaTh (m.)	کٹھ	he sheep, ram
kaDIna:vun (v.m.s.)	کڈہٕ ناوُن	to bring out, to turn out *kaDIna:vIn'*(m.p.,f..) *kaDIna:vIni* (f.p.)
kaDun (vt.m.s.)	کڈُن	to bring out, to bring forth *kaDIn'* (m.p.,f.s.) *kaDIni* (f.p.)

katIna:vun (v.m.s.)	کتہٕ ناوُن	to make spin *katIna:vIn'* (m.p.,f.s.) *katIna:vIni* (f.p.)
katIra:vun (v.m.s.)	کترٲوُن	to slice *katIra:vIn'* (m.p.,f.s.) *katIra:vIni* (f.p.)
katIrun (v.m.s.)	کَترُن	to slice *katIrIn'* (m.p.,f.s.) *katIrIni* (f.p.)
katun (vt.m.s.)	کتُن	to spin
kati (ad)	کتیٚ	where (locational)
kat'an (ad)	کتیٚن	where (locational)
katIra:vun (vt.m.s.)	کترٲوُن	to cut into pieces
katun (v)	کتُن	to spin
katrI (m.)	قطرٕ	a drop
kat'ath (ad)	کتیٚتھ	where (locational)
katinas (ad)	کتیٚنس	where (locational)
kath (m.s.)	کتھ	story, talk *kathI* (p)
kathIkuto:l (a.m.s.)	کتھ کتول	talkative *kathIkutA:l'* (m.p.) *kathIkutA:j* (f.s.) *kathIkuta:ji* (f.p.)
kathIgor (m.s.)	کتھ گوٚر	story teller
katha: (f.)	کتھا	narrative story with songs
kath k'uth (ad)	کتھ کیٚتھ	what for
kath ba:th (f.)	کتھ باتھ	negotiations, talk, chat
kad (m.)	قد	height

kadIr (m.)	قدر	respect
kada:var (a)	قداور	tall
kan (m.)	کَن	ear/ears
kanIvA:j (f.s.)	کنہٕ وآج	ar-ring *kanIva:ji* (p)
kan'a: da:n (m.)	کنیادان	giving away girl (bride) in marriage
kangan' (f.s.)	کنگنۍ	(a typical) lady's comb *kangIni* (p)
kanga:l (m.)	کنگال	bankrupt
kani shra:n (m.)	کنہِ شران	the bathing ceremony
kanz (m.)	کنز	mortar
kanzun (v)	کنزُن	to dress, to roast
kanzun (vt.m.s.)	کنزُن	to singe
kanTi:n (m.)	کنٹین	canteen
kanTro:l (m.)	کنٹرول	control
kand (m.)	قند	sugar candy in which direction, wherefrom *kapA:r'* (ad)
kapar tsa:dar (f.s.)	کپہٕ ژادر	bed sheet *kapar tsa:drI* (p)
kapar tsumIT (f.)	کپرٕ ژُمٹ	pinch for wearing new clothes
kapas (f.)	کپس	cotton
kapur (m.)	کپُر	cloth
kapTan (vi.)	کپٹن	cutting
kapTa:vun (vt.)	کپٹاوُن	to cut
kapta:n (m.)	کپتان	captain

kaphan (m.)	کفن	shroud
kabar (m.)	قبر	grave
kabarga:h (m.)	کبرگاہ	a meat dish
kaba:bI (m.)	کبابہٕ	grilled mincemeat
kabi:lI (m.)	قبیلہٕ	family, tribe
kabzI (m.)	قبضہٕ	control, occupation
kabrista:n (m.)	قبرستان	graveyard
kam (ad)	کم	less
kam (pr.p.)	کَم	who
kamar (m.)	کمر	waist
kamal (f.s.)	کمل	woollen blanket *kamlI* (p)
kam az kam (ad)	کم از کم	at least
kama:vun (vt.m.s.)	کماوُن	to earn *kama:vIn'* (m.p.,f.s.) *kama:vIni* (f.p.)
kamza:th ( )	کم ذات	mean, silly
kamA:y (f.)	کمٲے	earning, income
kamrI (m.)	کمرٕ	room/rooms
kami sa:tI (ad)	کمہِ ساتہٕ	at what time
kamzu:ri: (f.)	کمزوری	weakness
kamzo:r (a)	کمزور	weak, feeble
kay (f.)	قے	vomitting
kara:r (m.)	قرار	rest
kar (ad)	کر	when
kar (m.)	کرٕ	trunk of an elephant
karIna:vun (vc.m.s.)	کرناوُن	to make someone do *karIna:vIn'* (m.p.,f.s.) *karIna:vIni* (f.s.)

karam (m.)	کَرَم	deeds
karam bu:mi: (f.)	کَرَم بھوٗمی	field of activity
kara:kuli: (f.)	کَراکُلی	a type of round cap
kara:ma:th (f.)	کَرامٲتھ	miracle
kare:l (f.s.)	کریل	bitter gourd *kare:lI* (p)
karun (v.m.s.)	کَرُن	to do *karIn'* (m.p.,f.s.) *karIni* (f.s.)
karo:r (a)	کرور	one crore
karo:Dpati: (n)	کروڑپتی	millionaire
karzI (m.)	قرضہٕ	debt
kartal (f.f.)	کرتل	sword
kartu:t (m.)	کرتوٗت	deed, misdeed
karnal (m.)	کرنل	colonel
kal (f.)	کَل	deep desire, yearning
kalI (f.)	کلہٕ	head
kalIdo:d (m.)	کلہٕ دود	headache
kalIkhpIr (f.s.)	کلہٕ کھوپھر	skull *kalIkhapIri* (p)
kalam (m.)	قلم	pen
kalamda:n (m.)	قلم دان	penstand
kala:m (m.)	کلام	talk, speech
kala:y (f.)	کلاے	tinning, plating
kalash (m.)	کلش	Deity's symbol (a pot) worshipped on ceremonies
kalpu:sh (m.)	کلپوٗش	skull cap, a lady headwear
kalun (v.m.s.)	کَلُن	to stammer
kalun (vi)	کلُن	be dumb
kalshilavI (f.)	کلشِلو	sprinkling of holy water
kavI (ad)	کَو	why, for what reason
kavII' (f.)	کَوٕلۍ	a small cup *kavli* (p)
kashT (m.)	کشٹ	distress, pain
kashun (v)	کَشُن	to scratch
kashi:dIkA:ri: (f.)	کشیدکاری	embroidery (work)
kasIb (m.)	کَسب	art
kasun (v.m.s.)	کَسُن	to tighten *kasIn'* (m.p.,f.s.) *kasIni* (f.p.)
kasam drIy (m.)	قسم دٕرۍ	to take an oath
kasbI (m.)	قصبہٕ	town
ka:h ne:thIr (m.)	کاہ نیتھر	ceremony to purify the new born baby on the eleventh day of its birth
ka:kaz (m.)	کاکز	paper
ka:kaz varukh (m.)	کاکز ورق	a sheet of paper
ka:kaz k'om (m.s.)	کاکز کیوم	bookworm *ka:kaz kem'* (p)
ka:kaz sA:zi: (f.)	کاکز سازی	paperwork
ka~:gIr (f.s.)	کانگٕر	a Kashmiri fire-pot, brazier *ka~:gIri* (p)

ka:gza:t/ka:kza:t (m.p.)	کاغذات	papers
ka~:chun (vi.)	کانچھُن	to wish, to crave *ka~:chIn'* (m.p.,f.s.) *ka~:chIni* (f.p.)
ka:tsur (a.m.s.)	کاژُر	a person with brown hair *ka:tsIr'* (m.p.) *ka:tsIr* (f.s.) *ka:tsIri* (f.p.)
ka:j (m.)	کاج	button hole
ka:jvaTh (m.)	کاج وٹھ	grinding stone
k'a:zi (ad)	کیازِ	why
ka~:Tur (m.s.)	کانٹُر	he sparrow *ka~:Tar* (p)
ka:Th (m.)	کاٹھ	dry twigs, waste branches of a tree
ka:Thkarl (m.)	کاٹھ کرِ	fence
ka:tur (m.s.)	کاتُر	mule *ka:tar* (p)
ka:n (f.)	کان	mine
ka:ndur (m.s.)	کاندُر	baker *ka:ndar* (p)
ka:nul (m.)	کانُل	new leaves of sweede
ka:nul (m.)	کا نُل	a log bridge
ka:pi: (f.s.)	کاپی	note-book *ka:piyi* (p)
ka:preTu: (m.)	کاپریٹو	cooperative
ka:phi: (f.)	کافی	coffee
ka~:mbal ( )	کانبل	jaundice
ka:mida:r (a)	کامدار	embroidered
ka:yur (m.)	کایُر	pine timber
ka:v (m.)	کاو	crow
ka:r (f.)	کار	car
ka:rIba:r (m.)	کارِبار	trade, business
ka:run (v.m.s.)	کارُن	to boil *ka:rIn'* (m.p.,f.s.) *ka:rIni* (f.p.)
ka:rkun (m.)	کارکُن	worker
ka:rkha:nI (m.)	کارخانہ	factory
ka:ra:mad (a)	کارآمد	useful
ka:rtikh (m.)	کارتِکھ	Kartik - name of seventh month of Bikram calendar
ka:rna:mI (m.)	کارنامہ	deed, misdeeds
ka:l (m.)	کال	god of death
ka:lar (m.)	کالر	collar
ka:lcan (ad)	کالچَن	in the evening
ka:le:j (m.)	کالیج	college
ka:sh(tI)kA:ri: (a)	کاشتکاری	agricultural tenancy
ka:sun (vt.))	کاسُن	to shave
ka:sun (v.m.s.)	کاسُن	to cut *ka:sIn'* (m.p.,f.s.) *ka:sIni* (f.p.)
ka:sIna:vun (v.m.s.)	کاسہ ناوُن	to cause a cut *ka:sIna:vIn'* (m.p.,f.s.) *ka:sIna:vIni* (f.p.)
kikar kul (m.)	کِکر کُل	acacia tree *kikar kul'* (p)
kikar po:sh (m.)	کِکر پوش	flower of acasia tree

kitsh (ad)	کِژھ	for, what kind of
kitsh (ad)	کِژھ	little finger
kij/kIj (f.)	کِج/کٕج	peg
kiTh (m.)	کِٹھ	nicker, shorts
kita:b (f.s.)	کِتاب	book *kita:bI* (p)
kithIta:m pA:Th' (ad)	کِتھٕ تام پاٹھۍ	somehow
kinA·r' (f.s.)	کِنارۍ	margin *kina:ri* (p)
kipha:yath (f.)	کِفایتھ	economy
kima:m (m.)	کِمام	pride, boast
kirkaTh (m.)	کِرکٹھ	cricket
kira:y (f.)	کِرایے	rent, fare
kis (f.)	کِس	little finger *kisI* (p)
kih (f.)	کِہہ	waste hair
ki:nI (m.)	کیٖنہٕ	grudge
ki:myA:yi: pa:h (f.)	کیٖمیائی پاہ	chemical fertiliser.
ki:rtan (m.)	کیٖرتن	chanting of religious hymns
ki:val (ad)	کیٖوَل	only (one)
kemkha:b (m.)	کیمخاب	brocade
ke~h (ad)	کیٛنٛہہ	something
ke:k (m.)	کیک	cake
ke:n (m.)	کین	cane
ke:lI (m.)	کیلہٕ	banana
ke~:tsha: (n)	کیٛنٛژھا	anything, whatever
kudrat (m.)	قُدرت	nature, God
kul (m.)	کُل	tree *kul'* (p)
k'ul (m.)	کۄل	nail *kil'* (p)
ku~DI (m.)	کُنٛڈٕ	bolt
kun'ar (m.)	کُنِر	loneliness
ku~z (f.s.)	کُنٛز	key *ku~zI* (p)
kuTh (m.s.)	کُٹھ	a room *kuTh'* (p)
kuTh (m.)	کُٹھ	storehouse for grain
kuDIr (a, f.s.)	کُڈٕر	hard
k'ut/k'uth (pp.m.s.)	کۄت/کۄتھ	for *kit'* (m.p.) *kits* (f.s.) *kitsI* (f.p.)
k'uth (ad.m.s.)	کۄتھ	how *kith'* (m.p.) *kitsh* (f.s.) *kitshI* (f.p.)
k'uth ta:m h'uv (a)	کۄتھ تام ہیو	sad, feel áshamed
kutub kkha:nI	کُتب خانہٕ	library
kunItrIh (a)	کُنہٕ ترٕہ	twenty nine
kunItA:ji: (a)	کُنہٕ تاجی	thirty nine
kunInamath (a)	کُنہٕ نمتھ	eighty nine
kunIvuh (a)	کُنہٕ وُہ	nineteen
kunIvanza:h (a)	کُنہٕ وَنزاہ	forty nine
kunIshi:th (a)	کُنہٕ شیٖتھ	seventynine
kunIsatath (a)	کُنہٕ ستتھ	sixtynine

kunIhA:Th (a)	کُنہٕ ہاٹھ	fiftynine
kun zon (a.m.s.)	کُن زوٗن	all alone, *kun' zAn'* (m.p.,f.s.) *kun' zani* (f.p.)
kuni kuni (ad)	کُنہِ کُنہِ	sometimes
kuni kin' (ad)	کُنہِ کِنۍ	somehow
kuni pA:Th' (ad)	کُنہِ پاٹھۍ	somehow
kunisa:tI (ad)	کُنہِ ساتہٕ	at some time
kun tI ki:val (a.m.)	کُن تہٕ کیوٗل	all alone, single
kund' (f.)	کُنٛدۍ	iron (press)
kukil (f.s.)	کُکِل	cuckoo *kukilI* (p)
kunuy (m.)	کُنُے	alone
kubI (m.)	کُبہٕ	tomb
kumIla:vun (v.m.s.)	کُمہٕ لاوُن	melt *kumIla:vIn'* (m.p.,f.s.) *kumIla:vIni* (f.p.)
kumla:vun (vt.)	کُمہٕ لاوُن	to make tender
kurtI (m.)	کُرتہٕ	shirt
kursi: (f.s.)	کُرسی	chair *kursiyi* (p)
kul (m.s.)	کُل	tree kul' (p)
kul (ad)	کُل	on the whole
kuluph (m.)	قُلُف	lock
kulkoT (m.s.)	کُل کوٗٹ	trees and the like *kul'kAT'* (p)
kul' g~D (m.)	کُلۍ گونٛڈ	trunk of a tree
kulici (m.)	کُلچہِ	local bakery cakes, kind of bun
kul' dadIr (f.)	کُلۍ دَدٕر	a hollow in the tree, wood pecker
kul' phAki:r (m.)	کُلۍ فقیٖر	gypsy, nomad
kulham (a)	کُل ہَم	whole
kus (p.m.s.)	کُس	who, which *kam* (m.p.) *ks* (f.s.) *kamI* (f.p.)
kushti: (f.)	کُشتی	wrestling
kusu:rva:r (a)	قصوٗروار	guilty
ko:ThI (m.)	کوٹھہٕ	hut
ku:ch (v)	کوٗچھ	a call for a dog
ku:T (m.s.)	کوٗٹ	pole *ku:T'* (p)
ku:ThIr (f.s.)	کوٗٹھٕر	hut type room *ku:ThIri* (p)
ku:t (ad.m.s.)	کوٗت	how much *kI:t'* (m.p.) *kI:ts* (f.s.) *kI:tsI* (f.p.)
ku:t ka:l (ad)	کوٗت کال	how long
ku:n (m.)	کوٗن	corner
ku:r (f.s.)	کوٗر	a girl, daughter *ko:ri* (p)
k'u:r (m.s.)	کیوٗر	well *ki:r'* (p)
ku~:s (a.m.s.)	کوٗنٛس	youngster *ki~:s'* (m.p.) *ki~:s* (f.s.) *ki~:sI* (f.p.)

koc (a.m.s.)	کوٗچ	raw, unripe *kAc'* (p)
kotsh (m.)	کوٗژھ	bridge
koTh (m.s.)	کوٗٹھ	knee
kot (ad)	کوٗت	where
kot ta:m (ad)	کوٗت تام	upto what point
konD (m.s.)	کوٗنڑ	thorn
kob (a.m.)	کوٗب	hunch backed, hump *kob'* (m.p.) *kob* (f.s.) *kbi* (f.p.)
k'om (m.s.)	کیوٗم	insect *kem'* (p)
kom (m.)	کوٗم	husk
kor (m.s.)	کوٗر	a bangle *kAr'* (p)
kol (a.m.s.)	کوٗل	dumb *kAl'* (m.p.) *kAj* (f.s.) kaji (f.p.)
ko:phu:r (m.)	کوفوٗر	camphor
kokar tsa:s (f.)	کوکرٕ ژاس	whooping caugh
k>ru:p (a)	کورُوٗپ	ugly
k>rbA:ni: (f.)	قُربٲنی	sacrifice
ko:cI (m.)	کوچہٕ	lane
ko:cIva:n (m.)	کوچہٕ وان	horseman, coachman
ko:Th (m.)	کوٹھ	coat
ko:tur (m.s.)	کوترُ	pigeon *ko:tar* (p)
ko~:dI (m.)	کوٖنڈٕ	furnace, kiln
ko:n (a.m.s.)	کون	one eyed man *kA:n'* (m.p.,f.s.) *ka:ni* (f.p.)
ko:phtI (m.)	کوپھتہٕ	a meat dish, mince ball
ko:bu: (m.)	قوبوٗ	control
ko:m (m.)	قوم	nation, society
ko:mi: millItsa:r (m.)	قومی میلژار	national unity, amity
ko:r (ad)	کور	where
ko:r kun (ad)	کورکُن	in/to which direction
ko:l	کول	Kaul - a surname
ko:s (m.)	کوس	curve, arc
k>bun (vi.)	کوٚبُن	be hunch baked, hump
k>kur (m.s.)	کوکُر	cock kkar (m.p.)
k>kIr (f.s.)	کوکرٕ	hen *k>kIri* (f.p.)
k>kar pu:t (m.)	کوکرپوٗت	chicken *kkar pu:t'* (p) *kkar pu:ts* (f.s.) *kkar pu:tsI* (f.p.)
k>ch (f.s.)	کوچھ	lap
k>pheci (f.p.)	کوپھیچھ	ill-will, mischief *kpheT* (f.s.)
k>vo:k (m.s.)	کووۄک	who speaks some- thing inauspicious
k>ng (m.)	کونگ	saffron
k>ngI po:sh (m.)	کونگ پوش	saffron flower

k>pu:t (m.s.)	کوپۆت	prodigal son *kpu:t'* (p)
k>lay (f.s.)	کوٚلۍ	wife *klIyi* (p)
krI:l (n)	کرٟل	a worm, insect
krAhnIma:z (m.)	کرٛہنہٕ ماز	liver
kranz (m.)	کرٛنز	skeleton
kra:l (m.)	کرال	potter
kra:lI ba:y (f.)	کرالہٕ باے	potter's wife *kra:lI ba:yi* (f.p.)
kra:lI pan (m.)	کرالہٕ پن	thread of the potter
kra:y (f.)	کرائے	frying pan
kriya: karam (m.)	کریا کرم	funeral rites
kri:par (m.)	کریٖپر	creeper
kre~jul (m.)	کریٚنجُل	vegetable basket *kre~jil'* (p)
kre:char (m.)	کریٖچھر	bitterness, oppressiveness
kruh (m.)	کرُہ	two miles
kruhun (a.m.s.)	کرُہُن	black *krIhIn'* (m.p.,f.s.) *krihIni* (f.p.)
kru:d (m.)	کرۆد	anger *kru:r* (m.s.)well *kri:r'* (p)
kru:l (m.)	کرۆل	decoration of colours on the entrance of a house at auspicious occasions
kru:Th (a.m.s.)	کرۆٹھ	difficult krI:Th' (m.p.) *krI:Th* (f.s.) *kre:chi* (f.p.)
krotsh (n)	کروٚژھ	poker, a slough of a snake
krthI (m.)	کرتھہٕ	horse gram

kh

khIn' (f.)	کھنۍ	nasal mucus
khInzun (v.m.s.)	کھنزُن	to pull out hair *khInzIn'* (m.p.,f.s.) *khInzIni* (f.p.)
khipt (a.m.)	کھِپت	arrogant
khiptIgi: (f.)	کھِپتہٕ گی	arrogance
khIr (f.s.)	کھِر	slip *khIrI* (p)
khIsh (m.)	کھِش	scratch
khI:mI (m.)	کھیٖمہٕ	tent
khAjphal (m.)	کھجپھل	oil cake
khAzIr (m.)	کھزٕر	dates
khAzIr kul (m.s.)	کھزٕر کُل	date palm *khAzIr kul'* (p)
khArin' (f.s.)	خرٕنۍ	she ass *khArini* (p)
khAril (f.)	کھرِل	vulgarity, mischief
khAr'gi: (f.)	کھرٕگی	vulgarity, meanness
khAr'phI (a.m.)	کھرٕپھہٕ	naughty
khAhran (f.)	کھہرن	sharpness, sharpen, whet

khA:tIr (p.p.)	خاطِر	for
khA:dim (m.)	خادِم	servant
khA:r (m.)	خار	welfare
khA:ra:th (m.)	خارات	charity
khA:rij (m.)	خارِج	expel, dismiss
khA:rkha: (m.)	خارخاہ	well wisher
khA:li: (a)	خالی	empty
khA:siyat (f.)	خاصِیت	characteristic feature, quality
khac (f.)	کھچ	crowd, over crowding
khaca: khac (ad)	کھچاکھچ	full to the capacity
khajar (m.)	کھجر	breadth
khaza:nI (m.)	خزانہٕ	treasury, treasure
khAzA:n'ci: (n)	خزانچی	treasurer, cashier
khath (m.)	خط	letter
khatIm (n)	ختم	over, end
khatan ha:l (m.)	خطن حال	circumcision
khatarna:kh (a)	خطرناکھ	dangerous
khata:b (m.)	خطاب	address, title
khad (f.)	کھد	base, sustenance
khanIna:vun (v.m.s.)	کھنٕناوُن	to make dig, cause digging *khanIna:vIn'* (m.p.,f.s.) *khanIna:vIni* (f.p.)
khanun (v.m.s.)	کھنُن	to dig *khanIn'* (m.p.,f.s.) *khanIni* (f.p.)
khabar (f.s.)	خبر	news, message *khabrI* (p)
khabarda:r (m.)	خبردار	aware, beware
kham (m.)	خم	curve, bend
khamun (v)	کھمُن	panting
khay (f.)	کھے	ditch
khay (f.)	کھے	rust
khaya:l (m.)	خیال	imagination, idea
khAyA:li: (a)	خیالی	imaginary
khar (m.)	خر	he ass
kharI kharI (m.)	کھرٕکھرٕ	tickling
kharI sIh (m.)	خرٕسِہہ	tiger, panther, leopard
kharIc (m.)	خرٕچ	expenditure, spending
kharab (a)	خرَب	hundred thousand millions
khara:j aki:dath (m.)	خراج - عقیدت	homage
khara:b (a)	خراب	bad
kharun (v.m.s.)	کھرُن	to dislike *kharIn'* (m.p.,f.s.) *kharIni* (f.p.)
khargo:sh (m.)	خرگوش	rabbit
kharbuz (m.)	خربُزٕ	melon, musk melon
khal (m.)	کھل	place where harvested grains are collected, barn
khala:ph (m.)	خلاف	opposite, anti
khalun (v.m.s.)	کھلُن	to drive away (fly) *khalIn'* (m.p.,f.s.) *khalIni* (f.p.)

khav (f.s.)	کھَو	ditch (in which vegetables are preserved in winter) *khAv* (p)
khash kha:sh (m.)	کھش کھش	poppy seed
khasun (v)	کَسُن	to climb, to rise
kha:h (m.)	کھاہ	field
kha:kh (f.)	خاکھ	dust
kha:nI jang (m.)	خانہٕ جنٛگ	civil war
kha:nda:n (m.)	خانٕدان	family
kha:nyA:r' ha:kh (m.)	خانہٕ یارٕر ہاکھ	a variety of sweed
kha:nI vujA:Di: (f.)	خانہٕ وُجاڑ	destruction of a family
kha:b (m.)	خاب	dream
kha:m (a)	خام	raw, unripe
kha:mkha:	خامخاہ	without any reason
kha:mo:sh (a)	خاموش	silent
kha:mo:shi: (f.)	خاموشی	silence
kha:r (m.)	کھار	blacksmith
kha:run (v.m.s.)	کھارُن	to carry up *kha:rIn'* (m.p.,f.s.) *kha:rIni* (f.p.)
kha:l ka:~h (a)	کھال کانٛہہ	hardly anyone, scarce
kh'a:vun (v.m.s.)	کھیاوُن	to make someone eat, to feed *kh'a:vIn'* (m.p.,f.s.) *kh'a:vIni* (f.p)
kha:sIr(f.s.)	کھاسِر	skull
kha:skar (ad)	خاصکَر	especially
khetsIr (f.)	کھیتٕسٕر	cooked rice with lentils
khema: (f.)	کھیما	for bearance, apologise, mercy
khe:l (m.s.)	کھیل	play, game *khe:lI* (p)
khulI (a)	کھُلہٕ	loose, open
khulI DulI (a)	کھُلہٕ ڈُلہٕ	open, spacious
khulam khula: (ad)	کھُلم کھُلا	openly
khula: (m.)	کھُلاہ	divorce
khuma:r (m.)	خُمار	intoxication
khu:n (m.)	خوٗن	blood
khu:r (m.s.)	کھوٗر	razor blade *khu:r'* (p)
khu:tsIn'al (a)	کھوٗژٕنیل	coward
khu~:kh (a.m.s.)	کھوٗنٛکھ	one who speaks with nasal voice *khI~:kh'* (m.p.) *khI~:kh* (f.s.) *khA~:khI* (f.p.)
khu:prI (n)	کھوٗپرٕ	coconut
kh'on (v.m.s.)	کھیوٚن	to eat *khen'* (m.p.,f.s.) *kheni* (f.p.)
khoT (a.m.s.)	کھوٚٹ	base *khoT'* (m.p.) *khoT* (f.s.) *khci* (f.p.)
khot (m.s.)	کھوٚت	corner *khAt'* (p)
khonvaTh (n)	کھونٕوٕٹھ	elbow
khra:kh (m.)	خوٚراکھ	dose, food

kh>rdA:ni: (f.)	خوردنی	eatable things, edibles
khosh (a.m.s.)	کھوٚش	left hander
khoshi: (f.p.)	خوٚشی	happiness
kho~:khun (s.)	کھوٚنگھُن	long mouth of an animal
kho:j (m.)	کھوج	enquiry
kho:tsun (v)	کھوژُن	to be afraid, frightful
kh>:ph (n)	خوف	fear
kh>:phna:kh (a)	خوف ناکھ	dreadful
kho:l (m.s.)	کھول	kernel *khA:l'* (p)
kho:lun (v.m.s.)	کھولُن	to open *kho:lIn'* (m.p., f.s.) *kho:lIni* (f.p.)
kho:vur (m.)	کھووُر	leftside
kho:s (m.s.)	کھوس	cup *khA:s'* (p)
kh>car (a)	کھوچر	ill will, defect
kh>ji (m.)	خوجہ	an honorific title, tycoon
kh>Th (a)	کھوٹھ	defective, base
kh>D (m.)	کھوڈ	ditch
kh>DI k'om (m.s.)	کھوڈہٕ کیوم	an insect, a worm *khDI kem'* (p)
kh>dIpheci (f.p.)	کھوڈٕپھیچہ	mischief
kh>dkAshi: (f.)	خودکشی	suicide
kh>d mukhta:r (a)	خودمختار	independent, autocrat
kh>dgaraz (a)	خودغرض	selfish
kh>da:do:s (a)	خودادوس	God-loving, pious
kh>pIr (f.s.)	کھوپیٕر	cottage, hut evening, *dusk khpri* (p) *khphtan* (n)
kh>da: (m.)	خُدا	God
kh>r (m.)	کھور	foot
kh>rba:nI (m.)	کھوربانہٕ	a pair of shoes
kh>sh (a)	خوش	happy
kh>shbu: (f.)	خوشبوٗ	fragrance
kh>shIk (a)	خوشک	dry
kh>sh shAki:l (a)	خوش شکیل	handsome, beautiful
khra:v (m.s.)	کھڑاو	a wooden sandles *khra:vI* (p)
khrI~:ts (f.s.)	کھٕنژ	small mouse *khrI~:tsI* (p)

g

gIza: (m.)	غذا	food
gIshun (v.m.)	گیشُن	to rub
gIs (m.)	گیس	stools
gIhul (m.)	گٕہُل	thick, dense
gIhun (vt.m.s.)	گٕہُن	to g rind
gA~zrun (vt.m.s.)	گنٛزرُن	to count *gA~zrIn'* (m.p., f.s) *gA~zrIni* (f.p.)
gAb (f.s.)	گٕب	ewe *gabi* (p)

gAnzrun (vi.)	گَنٛزرُن	to count
gAzra:vun (vt.)	گنٛزراوُن	to count
gAr (f.s.)	گٔر	a watch *gari* (p)
gA~:Th (f.s.)	گانٛٹھ	a kite *gA~:TI* (p)
gA:n' (f.s.)	گانۍ	a prostitute *ga:ni* (p)
gA:phil (a)	غافِل	negligent
gA:nil (f.s.)	گانیِل	meanness, wickedness
gA:mi: (a)	گامی	rural, rustic
gA:ylI (n)	غایِل	accident, betrayal
gA:r (f.)	غار	water chestnuts
gA:rza:n (n)	غارزان	unfamiliar, unaquainted
gA:lib (n)	غالِب	name of an Urdu poet, predominent
gA:r hA:zir (a)	غار حاضِر	absent
gagur (m.s.)	گگُر	rat, mouse *gagar* (p)
gagra:y (n)	گگراے	thunder *gagra:yi* (p)
gach (m.)	گچھ	decoration
gatshun (v.m.s.)	گژھُن	to go *gatshIn'* (m.p.,f.s.) *gatshIni* (f.p.)
gaz (m.)	گز	a yard
gaTI (f.)	گٹہٕ	darkness, misery
gaTIka:r (m.)	گٹہٕ کار	darkness
gaTIpach (m.)	گٹہٕ پچھ	dark fortnight

gaTun (v.m.s.)	گٹُن	to decrease *gaTIn'* (m.p.,f.s.) *gaTIni* (f.p.)
gatshun (vi.)	گژھُن	to go
gaDI (m.)	گڈٕ	water pot
gaDur (m.s.)	گڈُر	goitre *gaDar* (p) *gaDIr* (f.s.) *gaDIri* (p)
gadIr (n)	غدر	injustice
ganI	گنہٕ	sugarcane
ganIts>da:h (n)	گنٕژہ داہ	Lord Ganesha's birth day
ganTi: (f.s.)	گنٹی	a bell *ganTiyi* (p)
ganTI (m.)	گنٹہٕ	an hour
ganTa: (f.)	گنٹا	a temple bell
ganDI (m.)	گنڈٕ	onion
ganDIna:vun (vc.m.s.)	گنڈٕناوُن	to get something tied *ganDIna:vIn'* (m.p.,f.s.) *ganDIna:vIni* (f.p.)
ganDun (vt.)	گنڈُن	to tie
ganDun (m.)	گنڈُن	betrothel ceremony
ganduk (m.)	گندک	sulphar
gandakDAb' (n)	گندک ڈٔبۍ	a match box *gandak Dabi* (p)
ganun (v)	گنُن	to deepen
ganun (vi.)	گنُن	become thick
gapshap (f.)	گپ شپ	chit chat
gabI (m.)	گبہٕ	applique

gam (m.)	غم	sorrow
gamgi:n (a)	غمگین	sad
garI (m.)	گرٕ	home
garIdivta: (m.)	گرٕدیوتا	house deity
garIba:r (m.)	گرٕبار	household
garIm (a)	گرٕم	hot, heat
garIve:Th (f.)	گرٕویٹھ	domestic property
garI garI (n)	گرٕگرٕ	door to door
garaz	غرض	essence, self interest
gara: (ad)	گرا	sometimes
gara:r (m.)	گرار	a dress
gara:j (m.)	گراج	garrage
garuth (m.)	گرٕٹھ	design
garun (vt.)	گرُن	to make, carve, to shape *garIn* (m.p.,f.s.) *garIni* (f.p.)
garkuli: (a)	گرٕکُلی	homely, domestic
gardan (f.s.)	گردَن	neck *gardani* (p)
garna:vay (f.s.)	گرناوے	mud washing of walls on the first day of the marriage ceremony among Hindus
garmun (vi.)	گرٕمُن	to become hot
gal (f.s.)	گل	cheek *galI* (p)
galath (a)	غلط	wrong
gala:zath (f.)	غلاظت	dirt, refuse
galun (vi.)	گَلُن	to melt
g'ag (m.)	گیگ	pharynx
g'av (m.)	گیٚو	ghee, clarified butter
gava:h (s.s.)	گواہ	witness
g'avIna:vun (v.m.s.)	گیوٚناوُن	to make sing *g'avIna:vIn'* (m.p.,f.s.) *g'avIna:vIni* (f.p.)
g'avangor (m.s.)	گیوٚن گوٚر	a singer *g'avangAr'* (p) *g'avangAr* (f.s.) *g'avangari* (f.p.)
gavarnar (m.)	گوَرنَر	governor
g'avun (v.m.s.)	گیوُن	to sing *g'avIn'* (m.p.,f.s.) *g'avIni* (f.p.)
ga:gIr (f.s.)	گاگرٕ	brass pitcher *ga:gri* (p)
ga~:gIlun (vi.)	گانٛگلُن	be disturbed, confused
ga:zIr (f.s.)	گازرٕ	a carrot *ga:zIri* (p)
ga:Tija:r (m.)	گاٹٕجار	intelligence, wisdom
ga:Tul (a.s.)	گاٹُل	intelligent, wise *ga:TIl'* (p) *ga:TIj* (f.s.) *ga:TIji* (f.p.)
ga:D (f.f.s.)	گاڑ	fish *ga:DI* (p)
ga:DIko~D (m.s.)	گاڑٕکوٚنڈ	a thorn of fish
ga:DIbatI (m.)	گاڑٕبتہٕ	the "fish feast" festival
ga:DIhA~:z (m.)	گاڑٕہانٛز	fisherman
ga:tuk (m.)	گاتُک	destroyer

ga:n (m.)	گان	a stable
g'a:n (m.)	گیان	knowledge
ga:nIva:n (m.)	گیانہٕ وان	prositiution
ga:ph (m.)	گاف	golf
ga:m (m.)	گام	village
ga:r (m.)	گار	a cave
ga:rat (m.)	گارت	guard
ga:l (a)	گال	shame
ga:lun (v.m.s.)	گالُن	to melt *ga:lIn'* (m.p.,f.s.) *ga:lIni* (f.p.)
ga:run (vi.)	گارُن	to search eagerly
ga:v (f.s.)	گاو	cow *gA:v* (p)
ga:sh (m.)	گاش	light
ga:shIliy (f.s.)	گاشہٕ لۍ	a ray of light *ga:shIlIyi* (p)
ga:shIta:rukh (m.)	گاشہٕ تارُکھ	the morning star *ga:shIta:rakh* (p)
ga:sI (n)	گاسہٕ	grass
ga:h (m.)	گاہ	light
ge:lun (vi.)	گیلُن	to make fun of
ge:run (vi.)	گیرُن	to surround
gid (f.s.)	گِد	dung of a calf
gindun (v.m.s.)	گِندُن	to play *gindIn'* (m.p.,f.s.) *gindIni* (f.p.)
gindIn:a:vun (v.m.s.)	گِندناوُن	to make play *gindIna:vIn'* (m.p.,f.s.) *gindIna:vIni* (f.s.)
gira:h (n)	گِراہ	sixteenth part of a yard
giriphta:r (n)	گرفتار	arrested
giriphtA:ri:	گرفتاری	imprisonment, arrest
girun (v)	گِرُن	to fall
girji (m.)	گِرجہٕ	church
girdI (m.)	گِردٕ	a kind of bread
gil (f.s.)	گِل	a kind of bird *gilI* (p)
gilvun (vi.)	گِلہٕ وُن	to whirl about
gila:ph (f.s.)	گلاف	cover
gila:s (m.)	گلاس	cherry
gila:sI (m.)	گلاسہٕ	a glass tumbler
gi:t (m.)	گیت	song
guch (f.)	گُچھ	a bunch
guzar (m.)	گُزر	octroi
guzarva:n (m.)	گُزروان	octroi man, collector of taxes
guza:rI (m.)	گُزارٕ	livelihood
guza:rband (m.)	گُزارٕبنْد	resourceful, rich
guza:răn (vi.)	گُزارُن	to pass time
guTInI (m.)	گُٹنہٕ	a kind of trousers
guda:m (m.)	گُدام	store
gudo:m (m.s.)	گُدوم	tether *gudA:m'* (p)
gunas (f.s.)	گُنس	a type of venomous snake *gunIsI* (p)

gunus (m.)	گنُس	a type of bangle designed as serpent's head *gunIs'* (p)
gunjA:yish (f.)	گنجایِش	scope
gupun (m.s.)	گپُن	an animal, cattle *gupan* (p)
guphta:r (m.)	گُفتار	talk
guba:rI (m.)	غُبارٕ	a baloon
gumI (m.)	گُمہٕ	perspiration
guma:nI (m.)	گُمانٕ	pride
guyun (n)	گیُن	rough grass
gur (m.s.)	گُر	a horse *gur'* (p)
guran (m.s.)	گُرَن	small fish *guran* (s)
gurus (m.)	گُرُس	buttermilk
gul (m.)	گُل	flower
gula:b (m.)	گُلاب	rose
gula:m (m.s.)	غُلام	a servant, slave
gulci:n (m.)	گُل چیٖن	a flower, plumeria alba
gulza:r (m.)	گُلزار	flower graden
guli aphta:b (m.)	گُلہِ افتاب	sun flower
gul'm'u:Th (m.)	گُلہِ میوٗٹھ	wedding present
gusI (m.)	غُصہٕ	anger
guh (m.)	گُہ	cowdung
guhul (m.)	گُہُل	thickness, dense
gu:j' (f.s.)	گوٗج	kernel *go:ji* (p)

gu:D (a)	گوٗڈ	difficult
gu:d (m.s.)	گوٗد	vagina
gu:r (m.s.)	گوٗر	milkmaid *gu:r'* (p)
gu:r'ba:y (f.s.)	گوٗرِ بایے	milkwoman *gu:r' ba:yi* (p)
g'u:r (m.)	گیوٗر	vertigo
gu:l' (f.s.)	گوٗلۍ	gunshot *go:li* (p)
goT (a.s.)	گوٚٹ	dim *gAT'* (m.p.) *gAT* (f.s.) *gaci* (f.p.)
got (m.s.)	گوٚت	weak *gAt'* (m.p.) *gAts* (f.s.) *gatsI* (f.p.)
god (m.s.)	گوٚد	a hole *gAd'* (p)
gon (a)	گوٚن	thick
gob (a.m.s.)	گوٚب	heavy *gob'* (m.p.) gob (f.s.) *gbi* (f.p.)
gobur (m.s.)	گوٚبُر	son *gobar* (m.p.)
gobIr (f.s.)	گوٚبرٕ	daughter *gobIri* (f.p.)
g>rdol (m.s.)	گوٚرٕدول	a sour fruit
gol (m.s.)	گوٚل	cheek, sip *gAl'* (p)
golA:b' (a)	گوٚلاٲبۍ	rosy pink
gola:bja:man (m.)	گولاب جامن	a kind of sweetmea

goshIbob (m.)	گوشہِ بوٚب	soft pears *goshIbAb'* (p)
gshta:b (m.)	گوشتاب	a meat dish
go~:tsh (f.s.)	گونٛژہ	moustache *go~:tshI* (p)
gon' (f.)	گوٚنۍ	a heap, rick
go:ya: ki (ad)	گویا کہ	as if
go~dur (m.)	گوندُر	bunch *gondar* (p)
go:r (m.)	گور	(Hindu) priest
go:rIba:y (f.s.)	گورِ بائے	wife of a priest *go:rIba:yi* (p)
go:l (a)	گول	round
go:sh (m.)	گوش	place
g>gIj (f.s.)	گوٚگِج	turnip *g>gIj* (p)
g>DI (ad)	گوڈٕ	at first, primarily
g>DIn'uk (a)	گوڈنِیُک	first
g>na:hga:r (a)	گوناہگار	sinful
g>nma:th (m.)	گونماتھ	an artist
g>bun (v.m.s.)	گوبُن	to be heavy *g>bIn'* (m.p.,f.s.) *g>bIni* (f.p.)
g>l (f.p.)	گوٚل	a crest
g>sI (m.)	غوصہ	anger
gr>tsun (vi.)	گرٛوٚژُن	to shake liquid in a vessel
grAhast (n)	گرٛہست	family
grAhasti: (f.)	گرٛہستی	home life
grI:s' ba:y (f.s.)	گرٛیسۍ بائے	preasant's wife, peasant woman *grI:s' ba:yi* (f.p.)
gru:s (m.s.)	گرٛوس	farmer *grI:s'* (p)
grakIna:vun (v.m.s.)	گرٛکہِ ناوُن	to boil *grakIna:vIn'* (m.p.,f.s.) *grakIna:vIni* (f.p.)
grakun (vi.)	گرٛکُن	boil over
grakIna:vun (vt.m.s.)	گرٛکہِ ناوُن	to boil *grakIna:vIn'* (m.p.,f.s.) *grakIna:vIni* (f.p.)
grazun (vi.)	گرٛزُن	roaring
grazun (v.m.s.)	گرٛزُن	to roar *grazIn'* (m.p.,f.s.) *grazIni* (f.p.)
graTI (m.)	گرٛٹہٕ	watermill, quern
graTIvo:l (m.s.)	گرٛٹہٕ وول	water miller *graTIvA:l'* (p) *graTIva:jan'* (f.s.) *graTIva:jini* (f.p.)
gra:ma:pho:n (m.)	گرٛاما فون	gramaphone
grad (m.)	گرٛد	vulture
gra~d (m.)	گرٛنٛد	count, numerals
gra:kh (m.)	گرٛاکھ	a customer
gra:m (a)	گرٛام	gram
gra:y (f.s.)	گرٛائے	movement *gra:yi* (p)
gruhun (m.)	گرٛہن	eclipse

c

cAr (a.f.s.)	چٕر	one who boasts *cari* (f.p.) *cor* (m.s.) *cAr'* (m.p.)
cA:nd' (f.)	چاٗنٛڈۍ	silver
cA:r (f.s.)	چاٗر	dumb *ca:ri* (f.p.) *co:r* (m.s.) *cA:r'* (m.p.)
cA:l' (f.)	چاٗلۍ	pride, mannerism
cak (f.s.)	چٕک	cheque *cakI* (f.p.)
cakIcak (f.)	چٕکہٕ چٕک	noise, shouting
canI (m.)	چنہٕ	gram
candI (m.)	چنٛدٕ	pocket, donation
canDa:l (n)	چنہٕ دال	cobbler, wretch
capIn' (f.s.)	چپنۍ	chapal, a footwear *capIni* (f.p.)
capIrA:s' (m.)	چپراٗسۍ	a peon
capkAl'	چپکٕلۍ	a kind of necklace
camkun (vi.)	چمکُن	to shine
came:li: (f.)	چمیٖلی	evening glory (flower)/jasmine
carIb (n)	چرٕب	fat
carsi: (n)	چرسی	one who is addicted to hashish or opium
cala:vun (v.m.s.)	چلاوُن	to drive *cala:vIn'* (m.p.,f.s.) *cala:vIni* (f.p.)
cashIm (f)	چشم	eye *cashmI* (p)
cahal pahal (a)	چہل پہل	hustle and bustle
ca:kh (m.)	چاکھ	chalk
ca:run (v.m.s.)	چارُن	to tighten *ca:rIn'* (m.p.,f.s.) *ca:rIni* (f.p.)
ca:y (f.)	چاے	tea *ca:yi* (p)
ca:rpa:y (f.)	چار پاے	a cot *ca:rpa:yi* (p)
ca:rvo:y (m.s.)	چار ووے	quadraped (animal), cattle *ca:rvA:y* (p)
ca:la:kh (a)	چالاکھ	clever
ca:vun (vt.)	چاوُن	to milk (cow)
ca:vun (v.m.s.)	چاوُن	to make drink *ca:vIn'* (m.p.,f.s.) *ca:vIni* (f.p.)
cikh (f.)	چیٖخ	cry
ciTh' (f.s.)	چِٹھۍ	a letter *ciThi* (p)
cina:cI (c)	چناچہ	because
cirgish (m.)	چِرگِش	noise of chatter
cil (m.)	چِل	peg, tent-pin
cilIbacI (m)	چِلہٕ بچہٕ	last 10 days of winter
cilamci: (n)	چِلمچی	wash pot (basin)
cilay kala:n (n)	چِلے کلان	first 40 days of winter
cilay khord (n)	چِلے خورد	second 20 days of winter
cilim (f.s.)	چِلم	hookah-bowl *cilimi* (p)

ci:n (n)	چیٖن	China clay
ci:rIna:vun (v.m.s.)	چیٖرناوُن	to saw, incise *ci:rIna:vIn'* (m.p.,f.s.) *ci:rIna:vIni* (f.p.)
ci:run (vt.)	چیٖرُن	to squeeze
ci:run (v.m.s.)	چیٖرُن	to saw, incision *ci:rIn'* (m.p.,f.s.) *ci:rIni* (f.p.)
ceTin' (f.)	چیٹنی	sauce
cumTI (f.)	چُمٹہٕ	hairpins, tongs
cust (a)	چُست	smart
curuTh (m.)	چُرُٹھ	a cigarette
cuka:vun (vt.)	چُکاوُن	to pay back, higgle-haggle
cu:~ki (c)	چوٗنکہِ	because
con (v.m.s.)	چوٚن	to drink *cen'* (m.p.,f.s.) *ceni* (f.p.)
co~cur (m.)	چوٚنچُر	adder's tongue
co:~khIra:vun (vi.)	چوٗنکھراوُن	to contract, to squeeze
co:kI (m.)	چوکہٕ	kitchen
co~:cI (n)	چوٗنچہٕ	ladle
co:n (pr.m.s.)	چون	your,yours *cA:n'* (m.p.,f.s.) *ca:ni* (f.p.)
co:r (a.m.s.)	چور	stupid, dumb *cA:r'* (m.p.) *cA:r* (f.s.) *ca:ri* (f.p.)
co:ras (m.)	چورس	a square, rectangular

ch

chAtIr' (f.s.)	چھتٕرۍ	an umbrella *chAtIri* (p)
chAtsIra:vun (v.m.s.)	چھٕژراوُن	to trouble someone *chAtsIra:vIn'* (m.p.,f.s.) *chAtsIra:vIni* (f.p.)
chakIr (f.)	چھکٕر	a Kashmiri group song
chakun (v.m.s.)	چھکُن	to scatter, sprinkle *chakIn'* (m.p.,f.s.) *chakIni* (f.p.)
chakra:vun (vt.)	چھکراوُن	to scatter
chakh (v.f.s.)	چھکھ	you are
chaTa~:g (m.)	چھٹانٛگ	one fourth of a pav
chaDI (a.m.)	چھڑٕ	an unmarried person
chati:si: (a)	چھتیٖسی	meanness, miserliness
chatun (vi.)	چھتُن	become white, to become grey
chanun (vi.)	چھنُن	fall from a mass, to be less
chanun (vi.)	چھنُن	be reduced, fall from (tree) *chanIn'* (m.p.,f.s.) *chanIni* (f.p.)
chanIra:vun (v.m.s.)	چھنٕراوُن	to cut *chanIra:vIn'* (m.p.,f.s.) *chanIra:vIni* (f.p.)
charun (vi.)	چھرُن	to deficate
chapun (vi.)	چھپُن	to be printed
chapun (vi.)	چھپُن	to scatter

chapar (m.)	چھپر	a roof
chaph (f.)	چھپھ	a great demand, hurry
chal (a)	چھل	piece *challI* (p)
chalun (v.m.s.)	چھلُن	to wash *challn'* (m.p.,f.s.) *challni* (f.p.)
challna:vun (v.m.s.)	چھلہٕ ناوُن	to make wash *challna:vIn'* (m.p.,f.s.) *challna:vIni* (f.p.)
cha:tI (m.)	چھاتہٕ	an umbrella
cha:n (m.s.)	چھان	a carpenter
cha:nun (vt.m.s.)	چھانُن	sift, trim, flail *cha:nIn'* (m.p.,f.s.) *cha:nIni* (f.p.)
cha:nIba:y (f.s.)	چھانہٕ بای	a carpenter's wife *cha:nIba:yi* (p)
cha:pIr (f.s.)	چھاپہٕر	(a kind of) hawker's basket *cha:pri* (p)
cha:vun (v.m.s.)	چھاوُن	to use, to enjoy *cha:vIn'* (m.p.,f.s.) *cha:vIni* (f.p.)
chetun (v.m.s.)	چھیٚتُن	to become old, (greying of hair)
che:kras (ad)	چھیکرس	at the end
chuTi: (f.)	چھُٹی	a holiday
chur' (f.s.)	چھُرۍ	a knife, dagger *churi* (p)
chu:t cha:t (n)	چھوٗت چھات	untouchability
ch>kh (m.)	چھوکھ	a wound
chot (ad.m.s.)	چھوٚت	grey *chAt'* (m.p.,f.s.) *chAts* (f.s.) *chatsI* (f.p.)
chon (m.s.)	چھوٚن	without, empty *chAn'* (m.p.,f.s.) *chani* (f.p.)
ch>kun (vt.)	چھوکُن	to wash
ch>mbun (v.m.s.)	چھومبُن	to thrash (grain) *chomblIn'* (m.p.,f.s.) *chomblni* (f.p.)
chAtsra:vun (vc. m.s.)	چھٕژراوُن	make white
cho:r (m.)	چھوٗر	thin cowdung
cho~:ph (m.s.)	چھوٗنپھ	churner *chA~:ph'* (p)
chindrun (vi.)	چھِندرُن	be to tremble
chivun (vi.)	چھِوُن	be impatient, be wild (with rage)

ts

tsI (pr.s.)	ژٕ	you toh' (p)
tsIn' (f.)	ژٕنۍ	a piece of charcoal *tsIni* (p)
tsInun (m.)	ژٕنُن	peach
tsInIn'kul (m.)	ژٕنٕنۍ کُل	a peach tree
tsInIn'po:sh (n)	ژٕنٕنۍ پوش	a peach flower
tsIhun (v.m.)	ژٕہُن	to suck *tsIhin'* (p)
tsIr (m.)	ژٕر	fraud
tsAnD (f.)	ژٔنڈ	blow, hit with (something)

tsA~dIr (n)	ژٔنٛدٕر	crescent
tsAndIrva:r (f.)	ژٔنٛدٕروار	Monday
tsAr (f.s.)	ژٔر	she sparrow *tsari* (p)
tsA~:gij (f.)	ژٲنٛگِج	straw mat, paillasse *tsA~:giji* (p)
tsakIj (f.s.)	ژکِج	anus
tsaki (ad)	ژکِہ	basically
tsakul (m.s.)	ژکُل	a piece, slice *tsakal* (p)
tsakh (f.)	ژکھ	anger, turf
tsaTIna:vun (v.ms.s.)	ژٹٕناوُن	to make cut, to effect cutting *tsaTIna:vIn'* (m.p.,f.s.) *tsaTIna:vIni* (f.p.)
tsasun (vi.)	ژسُن	laugh loudly
tsaTun (v.m.s.)	ژٹُن	to cut, to tear *tsaTIn'* (m.p.,f.s.) *tsaTIni* (f.p.)
ts'aD (n)	ژیڈ	patience
tsatIji: (a)	ژتجی	forty
tsa~dun (m.)	ژنٛدُن	sandal wood
tsam (f)	ژم	skin
tsamun (v.m.s.)	ژمُن	to shrink, decrease in size *tsamIn'* (m.p.,f.s.) *tsamIni* (f.p.)
tsamThun (vi.m.s.)	ژمٹھُن	to shrink, be stale
tsar (m.)	ژر	bed bug
tsarun (vi.)	ژرُن	increase
tsareth (a)	ژریٹھ	peculiar character

tsarna:mreth (m.)	ژرنامیٛرتھ	holy (water), ambrosia
tsal (vi.)	ژل	go away, get lost
tsalIra:vun (v.m.s.)	ژلٕراوُن	to chase someone away *tsalIra:vIn'* (m.p.,f.s.) *tsalIra:vIni* (f.p.)
tsalun (v.m.s.)	ژلُن	to run away *tsalIn'* (m.p.,f.s.) *tsalIni* (f.p.)
tsa:kh (a)	ژاکھ	four in one count
tsa:TIha:l (m.)	ژاٹہٕ ہال	school
tsa:Th (n)	ژاٹھ	pupil/pupils
tsa:dar (f.s.)	ژادر	blanket *tsa:dIrI* (p)
tsa:nIna:vun (vc.m.s.)	ژانٕناوُن	to make someone insert/enter *tsa:nIna:vIn'* (m.p.,f.s.) *tsa:nIna:vIni* (f.p.)
tsa:pun (v.m.s.)	ژاپُن	to chew *tsa:pIn'* (m.p.,f.s.) *tsa:pIni* (f.p.)
tsa:man (f.)	ژامَن	cheese
tsa:nun (vi.)	ژانُن	bring in, drive in
tsa:r (vt.)	ژار	to select, to choose
tsa:run (v.m.s.)	ژارُن	to clean, to select *tsa:rIn'* (m.p.,f.s.) *tsa:rIni* (f.p.)
tsa:l (f.s.)	ژال	palmful
tsa:lun (v.m.s.)	ژالُن	to bear, endure *tsa:lIn'* (m.p.,f.s.) *tsa:lIni* (f.p.)

tsa:lan (m.)	ژالَن	a wooden or iron piece used for stiring fire in Kangri (firepot)
tsa:s (f.)	ژاس	cough
tsith (f.)	ژِٹھ	backache
tsithIr (m.)	ژِتھٕر	Chetra (name of the 12th month) of Bikrami era
tsengun (vi.)	ژینٛگُن	to rejoice, make merry boast
tselun (vi.)	ژیلُن	to push in with force
tse:Tun (vt.m.s.)	ژیٹُن	to pound (to powder), crush *tse:TIn'* (m.p.,f.s.) *tse:TIni* (f.p.)
tse:nun (v.m.s.)	ژینُن	to feel, get a hint *tse:nIn'* (m.p.,f.s.) *tse:nIni* (f.p.)
tse:r (m.)	ژیر	late
tse:r (f.)	ژیر	appricot
tse:r paha:n (ad)	ژیرپہان	somewhat late
tse:rIkul (m.s.)	ژیرٕکُل	appricot tree *tse:rIkul'* (p)
tsuk (m.)	ژُک	sympathy, feeling
tsunamath (a)	ژُنَمَتھ	ninety four
tsupanjI (ad)	ژُپَنٛجہِ	(running) fast
tsuvanza:h (a)	ژُوَنزاہ	fifty-four
tsuvun (vi.m.s.)	ژُوُن	to fight, to quarrel *tsuvIn'* (m.p.,f.s.) *tsuvIni* (f.p.)
tsusatath (a)	ژُسَتَتھ	seventy four

ts'uh (m.)	ژیُہ	moment
tsuhA:Th (a)	ژُہَٹھ	sixty four
tsu~:Th (m.s.)	ژوٗنٛٹھ	apple *tsu~:Th'* (p)
tsu:r (a)	ژوٗر	thief
tsu:rim (a)	ژوٗرِم	fourth
tsok (a.m.s.)	ژوٚک	sour *tsok'* (m.p.) *tsoc* (f.s.) *tsci* (f.p.)
tsok (m)	ژوٚک	bottom
tsokIlaDar (m.)	ژوکہٕ لڈر	a local vegetable
ts>kun (vi.)	ژوٚکُن	be sour
ts>kun (m.)	ژوٚکُن	acidity
ts>kra:vun (vt.)	ژوکراوُن	be sour
tsuku~:jal (n)	ژُکوٗنٛجل	four cornered, rectangular
tsogun (a)	ژوگُن	fourfold
tsgIna:vun (vt.)	ژوگناوُن	make fourfold
tsoT (f.s.)	ژوٚٹ	bread, loaf *tsci* (p)
ts>mbun (vt.)	ژومبُن	to pierce
ts>mra:vun (vt.)	ژومراوُن	to decrease
tsop (m.s.)	ژوٚپ	bite *tsAp'* (p)
ts>pA:r' (ad)	ژوپآرۍ	everywhere, in all directions
tsor (m.s.)	ژور	extra *tsAr'* (p)
tsAr paha:n (ad)	ژٔرپہان	little more

tso~:g (m.s.)	ژونٛگ	small earthen lamp *tsA~:g'* (p)
tso:r (a)	ژور	four
tsovuh (a)	ژووُہ	twenty four
ts>th (f.s.)	ژوٚتھ	anus
ts>da:h (a)	ژوٚداہ	fourteen
ts>nzI (m.f.p.)	ژوٚنٛژ	servants
ts>y (f.s)	ژوٚے	conspiracy
ts>yitA:ji (a)	ژوٚیہِ تاجی	fourty four
ts>ytrIh (a)	ژوٚیہ ترٕہ	thirty four
ts>AyIshi:th (a)	ژوٚیہ شیٖتھ	eighty four
tsrAT (f.s.)	ژرٕٹ	a round mud wheel
tsIhun (vi.)	ژٕہُن	to suck *ts>h*
tshIrItsoT (f.s.)	ژھٕرٕژوٚٹ	a kind of pancake *tshIrIts>ci* (p)
tshAr (a.f.s.)	ژھٔر	empty *tshari* (p)
tshaTun (v.m.s.)	ژھٹُن	to winnow *tshaTIn'* (m.p.,f.s.) *tshaTIni* (f.p.)
tahaTIna:vun (v.m.s.)	ژھٹناوُن	to get winnowed *tshaTIna:vIn'* (m.p.,f.s.) *tshaTIna:vIni* (f.p.)
tshal (m.)	ژھَل	water wheel
tshalun (vi.)	ژھلُن	deceive
tsha~:Th (f.)	ژھانٛٹھ	swimming
tsha~:Dun (v.m.s.)	ژھانٛڈُن	to search *tsha~:DIn'* (m.p.,f:s.) *tsha~:DIni* (f.p.)

tsha:y (f.s.)	ژھاے	shadow *tsha:yi* (p)
tsha:l (f.s.)	ژھال	jump *tsha:lI* (p)
tsha:vIj (f.s.)	ژھاوٕج	she goat *tsha:vIji* (p)
tsha:vul (m.s.)	ژھاوُل	he goat *tsha:vIl'* (p)
tshen (v)	ژھێن	break, separation
tshenun (v)	ژھێنُن	to be torn *tshenIn'* (m.p.,f.s.) *tshenIni* (f.p.)
tshevun (vi.)	ژھێوُن	be extinguished
tsheph (f.s)	ژھێپھ	hide
tshey (f.)	ژھیے	grass used for house roof
tshevun (vi.)	ژھێوُن	be extinguish
tshevra:vun (v.m.s.)	ژھێوراوُن	to extinguish, to put out *tshevra:vIn'* (m.p.,f.s.) *tshevra:vIni* (f.p.)
tsheTun (vt.)	ژھێٹُن	be impure, unclean
tsheTIra:vun (vi.)	ژھێٹہٕراوُن	make impure, make unclean
tsh>tsun (vi.)	ژھوٚژُن	be empty
tsh>TIra:vun (vt.)	ژھوٚٹہٕراوُن	make short, shorten
tsh>TIra:vun (v.m.s.)	ژھوٚٹراوُن	to cut short *tsh>TIra:vin'* (m.p.,f.s.) *tsh>TIra:vIni* (f.p.)
tsh>Tun (vi.)	ژھوٚٹُن	be short, get short

tshunun (v.m.s.)	ژھُنُن	to wear *tshunIn'* (m.p.,f.s.) *tshunIni* (f.p.)
tshunIna:vun (vc. m.s.)	ژھُنہٕ ناوُن	to make someone wear *tshunIna:vIn'* (m.p.,f.s.) *tshunIna:vIni* (f.p.)
tshoT (a.m.s.)	ژھوٚٹ	short, pigmy *tshoT'* (p) *tshAT* (a.f.s.) *tsh>ci* (p)
tshoTin' (a.f.s.)	ژھوٚٹِنۍ	pigmy sized woman *tshoTini* (p)
tshop (a.m.s.)	ژھوٚپ	one who does not talk much *tshop'* (p) *tshop* (f.s.) *tsh>pi* (p)
tshor (a.m.s.)	ژھوٚر	empty *tshAr'* (p) *tshAr* (f.s.) *tshari* (p)
tsho:g (m.s.)	ژھوگ	pigtail *tshA:g'* (p)
tsh>kh (a.m.s.)	ژھوکھ	pride
tsh>tsI (f.p.)	ژھوژٕ	hollow
tsh>mb (f.s.)	ژھومب	tirck *tshmbI* (p)

j

jAlu:nI (m.s/p)	جلوٗنۍ	still (be) hot
jAgDI (m.s.)	جگڑٕ	quarrel
jAtsal (a)	جٔژُل	hairy
jA:li: (a)	جآلی	false
jA:ni: (a)	جآنی	fast, very close
jA:bir (a)	جآبر	curel, forceful
jA:yiz (n)	جایز	genuine
jA:ri: (v)	جاری	continuous
jakhun (v)	جکھُن	to work hard
jaD (m.)	جڑ	root, base
jamun (v)	جمُن	to freeze
jagar (m.s.)	جگر	a headwear, woollen skull cap
jaj (m.s.)	جج	judge
jaziyi (m.)	جزیہ	tax
jath (n)	جتھ	fur
jad (m.)	جد	forefathers
jadIbuD'bab (m.)	جدٕبُڈبب	great grandfather
jang (m.)	جنگ	war
jangju: (a)	جنگجو	war monger, quarrelsome
jangbAndi: (f.)	جنگ بندی	ceasefire
jangal (m.)	جنگل	forest/forests
jangla:t (m.)	جنگلات	forests
janath (m.)	جنتھ	heaven
jante: be:nazi:r (m.)	جنت بےنظیر	unique heaven
janu:bi: (m.)	جنوبی	southern
janvari: (m.)	جنوری	January
jabIr (m.)	جبر	compulsion

jama:h (m.) جمع addition

jama:th (f.) جماعتھ class
jamA:ts (p)

jama:da:r (m.) جمادار head sweeper

jamhu:riyath (f.) جمہوٗریتھ democracy

jarun (vt.) جرُن to deck with jewels

jara:si:m (m.) جراسیم germs

jarnA:l (m.) جرنیل general

jaljal (ad) جَل جَل immediately, fast

jalgo:zI (n) جَل گوزِ pine nuts

jalvI (m.) جلوِ glimpse, scenery

java:n (m.s.) جوان youngman

javA:ni: (f.) جوانی youth

javA:hir (n) جواہر jewel

jaha:lath (m.) جہالتھ ignorance

jA:girdA:ri: (f.) جاگیرداری feudalism

ja~:ch (parta:l) (v) جانچ investigation

ja:n (a) جان good

ja:niman (n) جانِ من own life, my dear

ja:nba:z (a) جان باز brave, daring

ja:nvar (m.) جانور bird(s),animal(s)

ja:n'ar (m.) جانیر goodness

ja:n pA:Th' (ad) جان پاٹھۍ very well

ja:phur (n) جافر marigold

ja:mI (m.) جامہ a dress, garment, gown

ja:mTri: (f.) جامٹری geometry

ja:y (f.s) جاے place, house
ja:yi (p)

ja:l (m.) جال net/nets

jigar (m.) جگر liver

jin (m.) جِن giant

jina:zI (m.) جِنازِ funeral procession (of Muslims)

jina:b جناب sir

ji:t (f.) جیت victory

ji:p (f.) جیپ jeep

ji:l (m.) جیل lake

jendIr' (f.s.) جیندرۍ trap
jendIri (p)

jeji:r (f.s.) جیجیر hubble bubble, hookah *jeji:rI* (p)

je:rI yun (v) جیرِن to be fed up

jukun (v) جُکُن to bend, to bow

judA:yi: (f.s.) جُدائی separation

judath (m.) جُدتھ bravery

juma:h (m.) جُمعہ Friday

jumlI (m.) جُملِ sentence/sentences

jurath (n) جُرتھ courage

jurma:nI (m.) جُرمانِ fine

julay (m.) جُلای July

juldI/jildI (m.) جُلد cover

ju:r' (f.s.) جوٗرۍ couple, pair
jo:ri (p)

ju:lI (m.) جوٗلِ swing

j>y (f.s.)	جوے	brook *jyi* (p)
j>ra:bI (m.)	جورابہٕ	woollen socks
j>la:bI (m.)	جولابہٕ	purgative
j>:kar (ad)	جوکر	joker
j>:rI (n)	جورٕ	two, second
j>:lnI (m.)	جولنہٕ	cloth bag
j>:sh (n)	جوش	zeal
j>:shi:lI (a)	جوشیٖلہٕ	zealous
j>thI (a)	جوتھہٕ	rough, ragged

z

zI (a)	زٕ	two
zIts (f.s.)	زٕژ	ray *zItsI* (p)
zIj (f.s.)	زٕج	red ant *zIji* (p)
zIto:vuh (a)	زٕتووُہ	twenty two fire fly *zitnik'om* (m.s.) *zitnikem'* (p)
zIl (m.)	زٕل	scratch
zIlun (vt.)	زٕلُن	to scratch
zAT (f.s.)	زٔٹ	an old cloth, rag *zaci* (p)
zAd' (m.)	زٔڈۍ	holes *zod* (s.)
zAn' (m.)	زٔنۍ	men, people
zAmi:r (m.)	ضمیٖر	nature, consciouce
zAmi:n (f.)	زمیٖن	earth, land
zAr (f.s.)	زٔر	deaf *zari* (p)
zAhi:n (a)	ذہیٖن	intelligent, wise
zAhi:rI (m.)	زہیٖرٕ	dysentry
zA:ts (f.p.)	زاژھ	castes, tribes, specic *za:th* (s)
zA:n (f.s.)	زان	basket
zA:n'ka:r (a)	زانۍکار	an acquaintance
zA:nith ma:nith (ad)	زانِتھ مانِتھ	knowingly, intentionally
zA:bitI (m.)	ضابطہٕ	genuine, in good teste, order
zA:miyi (m.)	زامِیہٕ	husband's sister's husband
zA:mi:n (m.)	ضامیٖن	responsible, guaranter
zA:r' (m.)	زارۍ	gambler
zA:lim (a)	ظالِم	cruel
zA:lda:r (m.)	زالدار	village headman
zA:v'ul (a.m.s.)	زاوُل	thin *zA:vil'* (m.p.) *zA:vij* (f.s.) *zA:viji* (f.p.)
zA:v'ja:r (m.)	زاوۍجار	fineness
zA:hir (ad)	ظاہِر	perhaps
zaka:th (m.)	زکاتھ	a religious rite of Muslims
zakh (m.)	زکھ	harm
zakhIm (m.)	زخم	wound
zag (a)	زگ	a dark red colour
zag batI	زگ بتہٕ	red coloured rice

zazur (a)	زَزُر	pale
zaTh (f.)	زَٹھ	matted hair
zaDIm~oD (a)	زڈِم ہوڈ	dull *zaDIm~oD'* (p)
zadIko:phtI (a)	زدِکوپھٹہٕ	severe beating
zan (ad)	زَن	as if
zana:n (f.s.)	زنان	lady, wife, woman *zana:nI* (p)
zana:nIzov (m.s.)	زنانہٕ زوٗ	womanish, one who likes the company of women only
zana:nId:d (m.)	زنانہٕ دود	female trouble
zang (f.s.)	زنگ	leg *zangI* (p)
zangItrey (n)	زنگہٕ ترٛے	a festival celebrated by Hindu women
zanji:r (f.)	زنجیر	chain
zanti (ad)	زنتہٕ	as if
zanD (m.)	زنڈ	bush
zab (f.)	زب	a kind of grass
zabar (a)	زبر	good, well
zabardas (a)	زبردستی	strong
zabikuk (m.)	زبہٕ کُک	a kind of bird
zaba:n (f.s.)	زبان	language, tongue *zabA:n'* (p)
zabehkha:nI (m.)	زبہہ خانہٕ	butchery
zAmi:n (m.)	زٔمین	land
zAmi:nda:r (m.)	زٔمیندار	cultivator, landlord
zAmi:ndA:ri: (f.)	زٔمیندٲری	cultivation, agriculture
zama:nI (m.)	زمانہٕ	time, period, era
zama:nath (f.)	ضمانتھ	security, bail
zar (n)	زر	money
zar (m.)	زر	fear
zarIka:say (f.)	زرِکاسے	a ritual of shaving off the hair of a child for the first time
zarIb (m)	ضرب	multiplication
zarIl'zA:j (f.s)	زرِلہِ زاج	cob web
zarar (a)	ضرر	harm
zarun (v)	زرُن	to bear
zarkIbarak (a)	زرکہٕ برق	brightness, splendour
zarmIsatam (f.)	زرمہٕ ستم	Lord Krishna's birthday
zardun (v.m.s.)	زردُن	to turn yellow, pale *zardIn'* (m.p.,f.s.) *zardIni* (f.p.)
zal (n)	زل	urine
zalur (n)	زلُر	spider
zalvun (a)	زلوُن	hot, warm
z'al (f.s.)	زٕل	layer, crest *z'all* (p)
z'av (f.s.)	زٕو	tongue *z'avI* (p)
zava:l (n)	زوال	downfall
zasud (n)	زسُد	zinc

z'avun (v.m.s.)	زٕوُن	to be born *z'avIn'* (m.p.,f.s.) *z'avIni* (f.p.)
zahar (m.)	زہر	poison
zapun (vi.)	زپُن	to pray
zazrun (vi.)	ززرُن	to dry up, to wither
za:th (m.)	ذاتھ	variety, caste
z'a:dI (a)	زیادٕ	more, much, extra
z'a:dI kh>ti	زیادٕ کھوتہٕ	at best, at most
z'a:dl (ad)	زیادٕ	
z'a:dI tar (ad)	زیادٕ تر	mostly, often
za:n (f.)	زان	acquaintance
za:nIvun (a.m.s.)	زانہٕ وُن	one who knows, knowledgeable *za:nIvIn'* (m.p.,f.s.) *za:nIvIni* (f.p.)
za:nun (v.m.s.)	زانُن	to know *za:nIn'* (m.p.,f.s.) *za:nIni* (f.p.)
za:phal (f.)	ژاوَل	mace, nutmeg
za:m (f.s.)	زام	husband's sister *zA:m* (p)
za:mtur (m.)	زامٕتُر	son-in-law *za:mtIr'* (p)
za:mut d>d (m.)	زامُت دوٗد	curds
za:r (m.)	زار	gambling
za:rIpa:rI (m.)	زارٕ پارٕ	to beg pardon
z'a:rath (f.s.)	زیارتھ	pilgrimage, holy place *z'a:rAts* (p)
za:l (m.)	زال	net
za:lun (v.m.s.)	زالُن	to burn *za:lIn'* (m.p.,f.s.) *za:lIni* (f.p.)
za:lIna:vun (v.m.s.)	زالہٕ ناوُن	to get burnt *za:lIna:vIn'* (m.p.,f.s.) *za:lIna:vIni* (f.p.)
za:la: di:vi: (f.)	زالا دیوی	goddess of fire
za:gun (vi.)	زاگُن	be watchful
zi (conj)	زِ	that
zikir (m.)	ذِکر	mention
zid (f.)	ضِد	enemity
zidi: (a)	ضِدی	stubborn, adamant
zina:h (m.)	ضِناہ	seduction
zindI (a)	زِندٕ	living
zindIdil (a)	زِندٕدِل	lively
zipI (f.p.)	زِپہٕ	to feel sleepy, drowsy
zimIva:r (a)	زِمہٕ دار	responsible
zimIvA:ri:	زِمہٕ وٲری	responsibility
ziy (a)	زِے	earning
zira:th (m.)	زِراتھ	agriculture
zilI (m.)	ضِلع	district
zi:kul (m.s.)	زیٖ کُل	earning hand
zi:Th (a.f.)	زیٖٹھ	long, tall *ze:chi* (p)
zi:n (m.)	زیٖن	saddle
zi:r (v)	زیٖر	push, touch, hint
zevIra:vun (vi.)	زیوٕراوُن	to cause to bring forth

zevun (vi.)	زیوُن	be born
zen (f.)	زیٖن	mud used for construction
zehan (m.)	ذہن	mind
ze:char (m.)	زیٖچھر	length
ze:Th (m.)	زیٖٹھ	Jyesht (name of the second month of Bikrami era)
ze:Thun (vi.)	زیٖٹھُن	prolong, lengthen, delay
ze:nun (vi.)	زیٖنُن	to conquer, to earn
ze:nun (v.m.s.)	زیٖنُن	to win, to earn *ze:nIn'* (m.p.,f.s.) *ze:nIni* (f.p.)
ze:bA:yish (f.)	زیبائش	makeup, decoration
ze:bra: (m.)	زیبرا	zebra
zuka:m (m.)	زُکام	flue
z'un (m.)	زیُن	fuel, cold
z'ur (m.)	زیُر	cumin seed
zuv (m.)	زُو	life
zulph (m.)	زُلف	hair
zulum (m.)	ظُلم	oppression, cruelty
zu:j (f.s.)	زوٗج	a part of particular headwear used by Kashmiri Hindu women *zo:ji* (p)
zu:j (f.s)	زوٗج	a wooden slate
z'u:Th (a.m.s.)	زیوٗٹھ	long, tall *zi:Th'* (m.p.) *zi:Th* (f.s.) *ze:chi* (f.p.)
zu:n (f.)	زوٗن	moon
zu:nIga:sh (m.)	زوٗنہٕ گاش	moonlight
zu:nIpach (n)	زوٗنہٕ پَچھ	lunar fortnight
zu:r (f.)	زوٗر	lamp stand
zu:l	زوٗل	illumination
zok (m.)	زۆک	pubic hair
zod (m.)	زۆد	hole
zon (m.s.)	زۆن	person *zAn'* (p)
zor (a.m.s.)	زۆر	deaf *zAr'* (m.p.) *zAr* (f.s.) *zari* (f.p.)
zo:tun (v.m.)	زوتُن	to shine *zo:tIn'* (m.p.,f.s.) *zo:tIni* (f.p.)
zo:r (n)	زور	force
zo:rI zo:rI (ad)	زورٕ زورٕ	quickly, loudly
zo:ra:var (a)	زوراوار	powerful
z~grun (vi.)	زٕنگرُن	be thin
z>sun (vi.)	زٕسُن	to caugh
z>n (m.)	زٕن	idea
z>pI (a)	زٕپہٕ	lazy, weak
z>mbI (a)	زٕمبہٕ	weak
z>lI (a)	زٕلہٕ	wink (of sleep)
z>v (f.s.)	زٕو	louse *z>vI* (p)

T

TIkun (v)	ٹکُن	to run

TAT' (f.)	ٹٹۍ	lavatory *Taci* (p)
TAT'b'o:l (m.s.)	ٹٹۍ بوٗل	cotton seeds
TAT'vo:l (m.s.)	ٹٹۍ وول	pony man
TA:c (f.s.)	ٹآچ	a kind of cap *Ta:ci* (p)
TakI (m.)	ٹَکہٕ	old two paisa coin
Tako:rI (n)	ٹکوٗرٕ	fomentation
Takh (m.)	ٹکھ	cut
Takun (vt.)	ٹکُن	to bite, to chew
Talun (vt.)	ٹلُن	to avoide
Tag (f.s.)	ٹگ	competition
TanDI (m.)	ٹنٛڈٕ	dispute, accusation
Tang (m.)	ٹانٛگ	pear
TangIkul (m.s.)	ٹانٛگہٕ کُل	pear tree *TangIkul'* (p)
Tab (m.)	ٹب	tub
Tama:Tar (m.)	ٹماٹر	tomato
Ta:sIra:y (ad.)	ٹاسٕراے	loud sound
Ta~:gIvo:l (m.s.)	ٹانٛگہٕ وول	a tonga driver *Ta~:gIvA:l'* (p)
Ta~:gun (vi.)	ٹانٛگُن	emit a loud cry, or roar
Ta:Th (m.)	ٹاٹھ	jute mat, coir mat
Ta:pas (m.)	ٹاپس	tops for ears, earring
Ta:lun (v)	ٹالُن	to avoid *Ta:lIn'* (m.p.,f.s.) *Ta:lIni* (f.p.)
Ta:s (m.)	ٹاس	thrash, cracker
TikaT (f.)	ٹِکٹ	a postal stamp, a ticket
Ti:n (m.)	ٹین	tin, can
TIsun (vi.)	ٹٕسُن	penetrate by force, force in
Ti:m (m.s.)	ٹیم	team
Tekin' (f.)	ٹیکِنۍ	horoscope abstract
Teksi: (f.)	ٹیکسی	taxi
Te:kIbaTan' (f.)	ٹیکہٕ بٹنۍ	adonis (a flower)
Tec (f.s.)	ٹیچ	dot *Teci* (p)
TeTh (a.f.s.)	ٹیٹھ	bitter *Techi* (p)
TeThun (vi.)	ٹیٹھُن	to turn bitter
Te:ng (m.)	ٹینٛگ	mound
Te~:Th (f.)	ٹیٹھ	false pride, snobbery
Te:bIl (m.)	ٹیبِل	table
Tukh (v)	ٹُکھ	cut
Tung (m.s.)	ٹُنٛگ	barking, howl *TungI* (p)
TubIra:y (f.s.)	ٹُبہٕ راے	beating of the drum
Tuvun (vi.)	ٹوٗوُن	close (eyes)
Tuvun (vt.m.s.)	ٹوٗوُن	to close *TuvIn'* (m.p.,f.s.) *TuvIni* (f.p.)
Tukun (vt.)	ٹُکُن	gnaw like a rat
Tu~:k (m.s.)	ٹُنٛکہٕ	a paisa, coin *TA~:k'* (p)
Tu:kIr (f.s.)	ٹوٗکہٕر	basket *Tu:kIri* (p)

Tu:p' (f.s.)	ٹوٗپۍ	a cap *To:pi* (p)
Tu:p'phol (m.s.)	ٹوٗپۍ پھوٗل	button *Tu:p'phAl'* (p)
T'ok (m.s.)	ٹیوٚک	tilak *Tek'* (p)
ToT (m.s.)	ٹوٚٹ	pony *TAT'* (p)
T'oTh (a.s.m.)	ٹیوٚٹھ	bitter *TeTh'* (p)
T'o~D (m.s.)	ٹیوٚنڈ	tip of the finger *Te~D'* (p)
Top (n)	ٹوٚپ	long hair
To:TI (n)	ٹوٗٹہٕ	pieces
To:Th (a.m.)	ٹوٗٹھ	dear one *TA:Th'* (m.p.) *TA:Ti:* (f.s.) *Ta:chi* (f.p.)
To:Thun (vi.)	ٹوٗٹھُن	be pleased
To:pigor (m.s.)	ٹوپہٕ گور	cap seller *To:pigAr'* (p)
To:r (m.s.)	ٹور	eyelid *TA:r'* (p)
To:lI (m.s.)	ٹولہٕ	family
To:li (f.p.)	ٹولہٕ	groups
T>kI (a)	ٹوکہٕ	strong, robust
T>ji (f.p.)	ٹوجہٕ	big eyes
Trak (m.)	ٹرٛک	truck
Trank (m.)	ٹرٛنک	trunk, box

Th

ThA~:Thur (m.)	ٹھاںٹھُر	brazier, maker of utensils
ThA:p'	ٹھاپۍ	an implement of potter
Thag (m.)	ٹھگ	swindler
Thagun (vi.)	ٹھگُن	be deceived, to swindle
ThaThI (m.)	ٹھٹھہٕ	joke
ThanDI (n)	ٹھنڈٕ	cold
ThAhrun (m.s.)	ٹھٲہرُن	to stop *ThAhrIn'* (m.p.,f.s.) *ThAhrIni* (f.p.)
Thahra:vun (vt.)	ٹھہراوُن	to stop
Thalun (vt)	ٹھلُن	to branch (a tree)
Tha:nI (m.)	ٹھانہٕ	lid, lids
Tha:sun (vt.)	ٹھاسُن	to drive in (a nail), to beat on head
Thi:kh (a)	ٹھیکھ	right, good
Thi:khpA:Th' (ad)	ٹھیکھ پاٹھۍ	well
Thikra:vun (vi.)	ٹھیکراوُن	to stand firmly
The:kI (m.)	ٹھیکہٕ	contract
The:kIdA:ri: (f.)	ٹھیکہٕ دٲری	contractorship
The:kIdar	ٹھیکہٕ در	contractor
Thukun (vt.m.s.)	ٹھوکُن	to fix, to press, to drive in *ThukIn'* (m.p.,f.s.) *ThukIni* (f.p.)
Thu:l (m.)	ٹھوٗل	egg, eggs

Th'ong (m.)	ٹھونگ	top of mountain, hill top *Thong'* (p) *Tho:kuridol*
Tho:s (a)	ٹھوس	concrete, strong
Tho:kur kuTh (m.s.)	ٹھوکُر کُٹھ	prayer room

D

DA:n (f.)	ڈائن	witch *DA:nI* (p)
DaknI (m.)	ڈَکنہٕ	lid
D'akI (m.)	ڈٮ۪کہٕ	forehead
DanDI (m.)	ڈَنڈٕ	stick, sticks
Dab (m.)	ڈَب	balcony
Damb (f.)	ڈمب	womb
Dal (f.)	ڈَل	land, field
Dalun (vi.m.s.)	ڈَلُن	to move, pass over, slide *DalIn'* (m.p.,f.s.) *DalIni* (f.p.)
Darun (vi.)	ڈَرُن	to fear
Da:kIvo:l (m.s.)	ڈاکہٕ وول	postman *Da:kIvA:l'* (p)
Da:ku: (n)	ڈاکوٗ	dacoit
Da:kh (m.)	ڈاکھ	mail
Da:kha:nI (m.)	ڈاکخانہٕ	post office
Da:kTar (m.)	ڈاکٹر	doctor, doctors *Da:kTar ba:y* (f.s.) *Da:kTar ba:yi* (p)
Da~:Tun (vi.m.s.)	ڈانٹُن	to rebuke, chide *Da~:TIn'* (m.p.,f.s.) *Da~:TIni* (f.p.)
Da:nas (m.)	ڈانس	dance
Da:y (a)	ڈاے	two and a half
Da:r (m.)	ڈار	small farm, dry land
Da:lun (v)	ڈالُن	to move, to shift *Da:lIn'* (m.p.,f.s.) *Da:lIni* (f.p.)
DIbIr (f.)	ڈِبہٕر	nut
Di:D'vo:n' (m.)	ڈیڈوانی	doorkeeper
DekIboD (a)	ڈیکہٕ بوڈ	lucky
Dejihu:r (m.)	ڈیجہ ہوٗر	a Kashmiri ornament
Desambar (m.)	ڈِسمبر	December
Delun (vt.))	ڈیلُن	be slack, be loose
De~:b (n)	ڈیٚنب	dumpy land, marsh
De:r (a)	ڈیر	heap
De~:shun (vi.)	ڈینشُن	to look, to see
DumDum (m.)	ڈُم ڈُم	drum beating
Dubun (vi.)	ڈُبُن	drown, sink
Duvun (v.m.s.)	ڈُوُن	to sweep *DuvIn'* (m.p.,f.s.) *DuvIni* (f.p.)
(m.)	ڈُل	big round pot
DulIna:vun (vt.)	ڈُلہٕناوُن	roll
Du~:gI (m.)	ڈونگہٕ	a big boat
Du:n (m.s.)	ڈوٗن	walnut *Du:n'* (p)

Du:n'kul (n)	ڈۄنۍ کُل	walnut tree
Du:mb (m.)	ڈوٗنب	a sweeper
Du:r (m.)	ڈوٗر	thread, cord
Do:l (n)	ڈول	drum
Do:lun (vi.)	ڈولُن	be unused
D>kun (vi.)	ڈۄکُن	fall half way, be weak *D>kIn'* (m.p.,f.s.) *D>kIni* (f.p.)
DD (۹)	ڈۄڈ	one and a half
Dra:ma: (m.)	ڈرامہ	drama

t

tItsh (f.s.)	تِژھ	a piece of cloth used for cleaning utensils/ floor
tIr (f.s.)	تٕر	a piece of cloth, rag *tIrI* (p)
tIlIr (f.s.)	تٕلٕر	wasp *tIlIri* (p)
tI:r (f.)	تیٖر	cold, shiver
tAkiyi (m.)	تَکیہِ	pillow
tAtsra:vun (v.m.s.)	تَژراوُن	to make hot *tAtsra:vIn'* (m.p.,f.s.) *tAtsra:vIni* (f.p.)
tA~du:rI (m.s.)	تَندوٗرٕ	oven
tAbiyath (m.s.)	طبیعتھ	health, welfare, temperament
tAmi:zI (m.)	تمیٖزٕ	good manners
tAhAr (m.)	تَہَر	cooked yellow rice
tAnra:vun (vt.)	تَنراوُن	to make thin
tA:ti:l (m.)	تأتیٖل	holiday
tA:mi:r (m.)	تأمیٖر	construction
tAmi:l karun (v)	تعمیٖل کرُن	to carry out orders
tA:r (ad)	تأر	time
tA:ri:kh	تأریٖخ	history, date
tA:ri:kh da:n (m.)	تأریٖخ دان	historian
tA:ri:kh nAvi:s (m.)	تأریٖخ نَویٖس	historian
tA:li:m (f.)	تألیٖم	education
tA:li:mi: markaz/ada:rI (a)	تألیٖمی مرکز / ادارٕ	educational centre/ institute
tA:v (f.)	تاو	frying pan
tA:vi:z (m.)	تاویٖز	amulet
tA:sh (m.)	تأش	provocation
tA:si:r (m.s.)	تأثیٖر	effect
tA:si:lda:r (m.)	تحصیٖلدار	tehsildar
tA:suph (m.)	تعصُف	prejudice
tA:hsi:l (m)	تحصیٖل	tehsil
takdi:r (m.)	تقدیٖر	luck, fate
takra:r (m.)	تکرار	clash
takli:ph (m.)	تکلیٖف	distress
takabur (m.)	تکبُر	pride
takhsi:r (m.)	تقصیٖر	fault, blame
takhsi:m (n)	تقسیٖم	division
tagun (vi.)	تَگُن	be known, make possible

tagun (v.m.s.)	تگُن	to know *tagIn'* (m.p.,f.s.) *tagIni* (f.p.)
tachun (v.m.s.)	تچھُن	to scratch *tachIn'* (m.p.,f.s.) *tachIni* (f.p.)
tanun (vi.)	تنُن	thinning
tajrubI (m.)	تجربہٕ	experiment, experience
tajvi:z (m.)	تجویز	proposal
taDap (f.)	تڑپ	restlessness
ta:Dun (vi.)	تاڑُن	be angry
tati (ad)	تتہِ	there
tat'an (ad)	تتٕتن	there (locational)
tatinas (ad)	تتہِ نس	there (locational)
tadbi:r (m.)	تدبیر	action, device
ta~drust (ad)	تندرست	healthy
tan (f.)	تن	body
tanab (f.s.)	تنب	ground floor of the house
tang (a)	تنگ	narrow
tana:zI (m.)	تنازٕ	quarrel
tapA:r' (ad)	تپأرۍ	in that direction
tapA:I' (f.s.)	تپأری	a kind of abuse
tapas'a: (f.s.)	تپسیا	meditation
taph (m.s.)	تپھ	fever
taphsi:l (m.)	تفصیل	detail
taphri:k (m.)	تفریق	difference, subtraction
taphri: pasand lu:kh (a.m.p.)	تفری پسند لوکھ	one who enjoys (sight seeing)
tabIr (f.)	تبر	a small axe
tabA:hi: (f.)	تبأہی	destruction
tabarda:r (m.)	تبردار	woodcutter
tabkI (m.)	طبقہ	class, category, group
taba:dul (m.)	تبادُل	exchange
taba:bath (f.)	تبابتھ	treatment
taba:h (f.)	تباہ	destruction
tabdi:l (m.)	تبدیل	transfer
tablI (m.)	تبلہٕ	a musical drum
tabsurI (m.s.)	تبصرٕ	commentary
tam (m.s.)	تم	rest
tama:h	طماہ	greed
tamA:hi: (a)	تمأہی	greedy
tama:shIgi:r (m.)	تماشہٕ گیر	spectator
tama:m (m.s.)	تمام	whole
tamun (m.s.)	تمُن	soot
tamo:k (m.)	تموک	tobacco
tambIr (m.)	تمبر	tamarind
tamblun (vi.)	تمبلُن	to be impatient
tambIla:vun (v.m.s.)	تمبلاوُن	to tempt, to attract *tambIla:vIn'* (m.p.,f.s.) *tambIla:vIni* (f.p.)
tazkirI (m.)	تذکرٕ	mention
tayA:ri: (f.)	تیأری	readiness, preparation

taya:r (a)	تیار	ready
tar (m.)	تر	sprout, result
taraph (ad)	طرف	side
tAri:kI (m.)	طریقہ	method
tarun (v.m.s.)	ترُن	to cross *tarIn'* (m.p.,f.s.) *tarIni* (f.p.)
tatun (vi.)	تتُن	to become hot
tapun (vi.)	تپُن	take for the sake of warmth
tarkA:r' (f.)	ترکاری	vegetable dish
taraki: (f.)	ترقی	progress
taraki:pasand (a)	ترقی پسند	progressive minded
tarki:ya:phtI (a)	ترقی یافتہ	developed
tarngI (m.s.)	ترنگہ	typical headgear used by Hindu women
tarjamI (m.)	ترجمہ	translation
tarz (m.)	طرز	fashion, way, tune
tarta:zI (a)	ترتازٕ	fresh
tarbiyath (m.)	تربیتھ	training
tarsun (v)	ترسُن	to strive, crave
tal (pp.)	تل	under
tallna:vun (v)	تلہِ ناوُن	to get fried (by someone) *tallna:vIn'* (m.p.,f.s.) *tallna:vIni* (f.p.)
talA:shi: (f.)	تلاشی	search (warrent)
tala:sh	تلاش	search

talab (m.)	طلب	requirement, need
talun (v.m.s.)	تلُن	to fry *tallIn'* (m.p.,f.s.) *tallIni* (f.p.)
talpod (m.s.)	تلہِ پوٚد	sole *talpAd'* (m.p.)
tavay (ad)	توٕے	that is why, for that reason
tavIna:vun (v.m.s.)	توٕناوُن	to get baked, to roast *tavIna:vIn'* (m.p.,f.s.) *tavIna:vIni* (f.p.)
tavun (v.m.s.)	توٕن	to bake, to roast *tavIn'* (m.p.,f.s.) *tavIni* (f.p.)
tavkal (m.)	توکل	belief, trust in God
tashtAr' (f.s.)	طشتری	tray *tashtari* (p)
tas (pr)	تس	to him/to her
tasla: (f.)	تسلا	satisfaction, consolation
ta:h (m.)	تہہ	layer
tahki:ka:t (m.s.)	تحقیقات	investigation
tahki:k (m.)	تحقیک	research
ta:kaya:math (ad)	تا قیامتھ	till doomsday
taha:rath (m.)	تحارتھ	courage, guts, ablution
tahband (m.)	تہہ بند	petticoat, leg sheet
ta:ki (c)	تاکہ	so that
ta:khuc (m.s.)	تاقچہ	niche, shelf in a wall *ta:khIc* (p)

ta:kh (m)	تاکھ	window
ta:kh (a)	تاکھ	odd number
ta:j (m.s.)	تاج	crown
ta:ph (m.)	تاپھ	sunlight
ta:b (m.)	تاب	patience
ta:m (pp.)	تام	till, upto, for sometime (now)
ta:n' (pp.)	تانٛ	till, upto
ta:r (f.s.)	تار	telegram, wire *ta:rI* (p)
ta:rI (a)	تارٕ	three
ta:rukh (f.s)	تارٕکھ	star *ta:rakh* (p)
ta:run (vt.)	تارُن	pass over, cross (a river)
ta:rko:l (m.)	تارکول	coaltar
ta:rgar (m.)	تارگر	telegraph office
ta:l (f.s.)	تال	rythm
ta:lIraz (f.)	تالہٕ رز	an ornament
ta:lav (f.)	تالو	ceiling of house
ta:la:b (m.)	تالاب	pond
ta:van (m.)	تاوَن	plague, an abuse
ta:vIhot (a)	تاوٕہۆت	draughtful, dry with heat
ta:vanzad (n)	تاوَن زد	an abuse, plagued (man)
ta:shva:n (m.)	تاشوان	prostitution
ta:s (m.)	تاس	playing cards
tik'a:zi	تِکیازِ	because
tiku:n (m.)	تِکوٗن	triangle
tikh (a.)	تِکھ	piece (of meat)
tiphII (m.)	تِفلہٕ	immature, naughty
tib (f.s.)	طِب	system of medicine
tihund (pro.m.s.)	تِہُنٛد	their *tihInd'* (p) *tihInz* (f.s.) *tihInzI* (f.p.)
tihur (m.s.)	تِہُر	tree top, top *tihIr'* (p)
ti:t'	تیٖتۍ	so many
ti:z (m.s.)	تیٖز	glamour
ti:r (f.)	تیٖر	feather, arrow
ti:rath (m.)	تیٖرتھ	holy place
ti:l (m.)	تیٖل	oil
ti:lIp'ot (m.s.)	تیٖلہٕ پۆت	gall bladder *ti:lIpet'* (p)
ti:lIvA:r (m.)	تیٖلہٕ وٲر	oil pot
tilIvo:n' (m.)	تیٖلہٕ وونۍ	oilman
ti:lIsaDakh (f.)	تیٖلہٕ سڑک	metalled road
tembIr (m.)	تیمبٕر	spark
teyitA:ji: (a)	تیٚیہٕ تٲجی	forty three
teli (ad)	تیلہِ	then
teyitrIh (a)	تیٚیہٕ ترٕہ	thirty three
te:z (ad)	تیز	sharp
te:z te:z (ad)	تیز تیز	quickly
te:zun (vi.)	تیزُن	be sharp, be provoked
te:zIra:vun (vt.)	تیزٕراوُن	to sharpen, to provoke

te:da:d (m.)	تیداد	count, number
te:l (m.)	تیل	sesame
t'uth (ad)	تیُتھ	that type of
t'uthuy (ad)	تیُتھٕے	at that very moment
tumbakhnA:r (f.s.)	تُمبکھناًر	a musical instrument *tumakhna:ri* (p)
tul (m.)	تُل	mulberry
tulun (v.m.s.)	تُلُن	to pick up, to lift *tulIn'* (m.p.,f.s.) *tulIni* (f.p.)
tulIna:vun (v.m.s.)	تُلہٕ ناوُن	to get lifted *tulIna:vIn'* (m.p.,f.s.) *tulIna:vIni* (f.p.)
tulIkul (m.s.)	تُلہٕ کُل	mulberry tree *tulIkul'* (p)
tuhund (pr.m.s.)	تُہُنٛد	your *tuhInd'* (p) *tuhInz* (f.s.) *tuhInzI* (p)
turun (a.m.s.)	تُرُن	cold *tIrIn'* (m.p.,f.s.) *tIrIni* (f.p.)
tulkatur (m.)	تُلہٕ کتُر	ice
tu:n (m.s.)	توٗن	navel *tu:n'* (p)
tu:r (f.s.)	توٗر	adze *to:ri* (p)
t'u:r (m.s.)	تیوٗر	sheep *ti:r'* (p)
togmI (m.)	توٚگمہٕ	medal
tot (ad)	توٚت	there (directional), hot
tot ta:m (ad)	توٚت تام	upto that point
ton (a.m.s.)	توٚن	thin *tAn'* (m.p.,f.s.) *tani* (f.p.)
t'ongul (m.s.)	تیوٚنگُل	live charcoal *tengal* (p)
tobrukh (m.)	توٚبرُکھ	gift, benediction
tomul (m.)	توٚمُل	rice
tomb (f.s.)	توٚنب	cotton flake *tomb'* (p)
tomlItsoT (m.s.)	توٚملہٕ ژوٚٹ	rice bread *tomlItsci* (p)
to~:th (f.s.)	توٚنٛتھ	beak *to~:tl* (p)
to:tI (m.)	طوطہٕ	parrot/parrots
to:ti (ad)	توتِہ	even then
to:r (ad)	تور	there (directional)
to:r kun (ad)	تورکُن	in that direction
to:lI (m.)	تولہٕ	a tola - a unit of weight
to:lun (v.m.s.)	تولُن	to weigh *to:lIn'* (m.p.,f.s.) *to:lIni* (f.p.)
to:lukh (m.)	تولُق	relation
to:liya: (m.)	تولِیا	towel
to:shkha:nI (m.)	توشہٕ خانہٕ	state furnishing department
to:shun (vi.)	توشُن	be happy
t>h (m.)	توٗہ	husk
trIh (a)	ترٛہ	thirty
trIhim (a)	ترٛہِم	thirtieth

trakIr (f.s.)	ترٛکِر	scale *trakIri* (p)
trakur (a.m.s.)	ترٛکُر	stiff, hard *trakIr'* (p) *trakur* (f.s.) *trakIri* (f.p.)
trakrun (vi.)	ترٛکرُن	be hard, harden
trakra:vun (vt.)	ترٛکراوُن	make hard
trakh (a.)	ترٛکھ	approx five kilograms
traTh (f.s.)	ترٛٹھ	thundering bolt
tra:m (m.)	ترٛام	copper
tra:vun (v.m.s.)	ترٛاوُن	to leave, to throw, to lay *tra:vIn'* (m.p.,f.s.) *tra:vIni* (f.p.)
tra:vun (vt.)	ترٛاوُن	let go
tra:vIna:vun (v.m.s.)	ترٛاوِناوُن	to get thrown *tra:vIna:vIn'* (m.p.f.s.) *tra:vIna:vIni* (f.p.)
tratsun (vi.)	ترٛژُن	fear, to get bored, be disturbed
tratsra:vun (vi.)	ترٛژراوُن	cause fear, to bore, to disturb
tre (a)	ترٛے	three
trogun (a)	ترٛوٗگُن	three fold
treyim (a)	ترٛیِیم	third
treyishi:th (a)	ترٛیِشیٖتھ	eighty three
trA:l (f.s.)	ترٛأل	(a variety) of small apple *trA:lI* (p)
tre:sh (f.s.)	ترٛیش	drinking water
tre:shIhot (a. m.s.)	ترٛیشہِ ہوٚت	thirsty *tre:shIhAt'* (p) *tre:shIhAts* (f.s.) *tre:shIhatsI* (f.p.)
tre:shun (v.m.s.)	ترٛیشُن	to strive, to crave *tre:shIn'* (m.p.,f.s.) *tre:shIni* (f.p.)
trukun (v.m.s.)	ترٛکُن	to cut with teeth *trukIn'* (m.p.,f.s.) *trukIni* (f.p.)
trukun (vt.)	ترٛکُن	to cut to pieces
trunamath (a)	ترٛنمتھ	ninety three
truvanza:h (a)	ترٛونزاہ	fifty three
truva:h (a)	ترٛواہ	thirteen
trusatath (a)	ترٛستتھ	seventy three
truhA:Th (a)	ترٛہاٹھ	sixty three
trombun (vt.)	ترٛومبُن	to prick, inoculate
tropIrun (v)	ترٛوپِرُن	to fill, to sew
trosh (a)	ترٛوش	crisp
trovuh (a)	ترٛووُہ	twenty three
tro:run (vi.)	ترٛورُن	be hardened (of an open boil, cut etc.)
tr>shun (vi.)	ترٛوشُن	become hard, crisp
tr>shra:vun (vc.)	ترٛوشراوُن	make hard

th

thAjka:d (m.)	تھٔجکاد	plantation of paddy
thAn' (f.)	تھٔنۍ	butter

thAr (f.s.)	تھٕر	bush *thari* (p)
thA:l' (f.s.)	تھٲلؠ	plate *tha:li* (p)
thakh (n)	تھَکھ	rest
thaka:vaTh (f.)	تھکاوٹھ	tiredness
thadun (vi.)	تھدُن	be high, go higher
thakun (vi.m.s.)	تھکُن	to get tired *thakIn'* (m.p.,f.s.) *thakIni* (f.p.)
thaph din' (v)	تھپھ دِنؠ	to snatch, catch, grab
thamb (m.s.)	تھمب	pillar
thar (f.)	تھٔر	back
thal (f.)	تھل	plants for plantation
thavun (v.m.s.)	تھوُن	to keep *thavIn'* (m.p.,f.s.) *thavIni* (f.p.)
thazrun (vi.)	تھزرُن	be high, go higher
thazra:vun (vt.)	تھزراوُن	make high
thamun (vi.)	تھمُن	be at rest, come to rest
thar atsIn' (vi.)	تھر اژنؠ	to tremble, shiver
thavun (vi.)	تھوُن	to keep
tha:n (m.)	تھان	role of cloth
tha:nI (m.)	تھانہٕ	police station
tha:pIr (f.s.)	تھاپٕر	slap *tha:pri* (p)
tha:ph (v)	تھاپھ	patting
tha:mun (v)	تھامُن	to stop
tha:l (m.)	تھال	a plate
tha~:thIrun (vi.)	تھاںتھرُن	be nervous
thekun (vi.)	تھیٚکُن	to boast
thurun (vt.)	تھُرُن	to make (a pot)
thog (m.s.)	تھوٚگ	broken branch *thog'* (p)
thod (m.)	تھوٚد	tall *thAd'* (m.p.) *thAz* (f.s.) *thazI* (f.p.)
thop (v.m.s.)	تھوٚپ	block *thop'* (p)
thos (m.s.)	تھوٚس	flake of snow *thos'* (p)
tho~b (m.s.)	تھوٚنب	handful (of liquid) *tho~b'* (p)
th>kh (f.s.)	تھۄکھ	spittle *th>kI* (p)
th>s (f.)	تھۄس	obstacle, embarassment

d

dInun (vi.)	ڈٕنُن	to shake out dust, disperse
dIy (f.s.)	ڈٕے	hatred
dIyun (v.m.)	ڈٕیُن	to be sorrowful
dIh (m.s.)	ڈٕہ	smoke
dInIra:vun (v.m.s.)	ڈٕنٕراوُن	to shake, to weaken, to harass *dInIra:vIn'* (m.p.,f.s.) *dInIra:vIni* (f.p.)

dAchun (m.s.)	دٕچھُن	right side *dAchIn'* (p)
dAdra:vun (vt.)	دُدراوُن	make weak, weaken
dAj (f.s.)	دٕج	handkerchief, piece of cloth *daji* (p)
dAndIr (f.s.)	دٕنٛدٕر	edge *dAndIri* (p)
dAr (a.f.s.)	دٕر	strong
dArindI (m.)	دٕرِنٛدٕ	wild animal
dAs (pp.)	دٕسی	by, through
dAsil (m.)	دٕسِل	mason
dAsti: (ad)	دٕستی	at the very moment, by hand
dAsla:bI (n)	دٕسلابہٕ	beginning, income from the first sale in the day
dAsh (f.s.)	دٕش	vative rag *dashi* (p)
dAh (a)	دٕہ	ten
dAhim (a)	دٕہِم	tenth
dAhim d>h (m.)	دٕہِم دوہ	tenth day ceremony after death
dA:khlI (m.)	دأخِل	admission
dA~:t (m.)	دأنٛت	ivory
dA~:tun (m.s.)	دأنٛتُن	a kind of teeth cleaner *dA~:tan* (p)
dA:d'lad (m.)	دأدِ لد	sick, ailing
dA:n (m.s/p)	دأن	pomegranate
dA:n kuj (f.s.)	دأن کُج	pomegranate tree
dA:n po:sh (m.)	دأن پوش	pomegranate blossom
dA:n' (a.f.s.)	دأنۍ	a little, gram *da:ni* (p)
dAn'ra:vun (vt.)	دٕنۍراوُن	consider, reflect, think
dA:r (m.s.)	دأر	window *da:ri* (p)
dA:r (f.)	دأر	beard
da:run (vi.)	دارُن	to owe
dakI (v)	دکہٕ	push
dakh'un (m.s.)	دکھیُن	south
dakhina: (m.)	دکھنا	money paid to the priest
dag (m.)	دَگ	pain
daga:ba:z (a)	دغاباز	cheat
dagun (v)	دگُن	to beat, pound
dagda:r (a)	دَگ دار	painstaking
dach (m.)	دٕچھ	grapes
dazun (v.m.s.)	دزُن	to burn *dazIn'* (m.p.,f.s.) *dazIni* (f.p.)
datur (m.)	دتُر	thorn apple, stramonium
datIr'kul (m.s.)	دتٕرۍکُل	thorn apple (plant) *datIr'kul'* (p)
dadIr (f.)	ددٕر	ripe cucumber
dand (m.)	دنٛد	tooth, teeth
dand sa:z (m.)	دنٛدساز	dentist

dangal (f.s.)	دنگل	wrestling
dapun (v)	دپن	to say
daphtar (m.)	دفتر	office
dabIdab (m.)	دبہ دب	wrestling
daba:vun (vt.)	دباون	to press down,crush
damIT'oTh (m.)	دمہ ٹھوٗٹھ	strong black tea
daman bastI (m.)	دمن بستہٕ	bellows
damun (vi.)	دمُن	to hollow, gasp
damo:luv (m.)	دمہ اولُو	a potato dish
damdA:r (f.s.)	دم دار	parapet, threshold
damda:r (m.)	دم دار	strong, serious
damcu:lI (m.)	دم چوٗلہٕ	small charcoal stove
darun (vi.)	درُن	be steady, stop
day (m.)	دَے	God
daya:h (f.s.)	دیاہ	courtesy, mercy
darIj (m.)	درٕج	admission, include
darId (m.)	درٕد	pain, feeling
darIm (m.)	درٕم	faith
darasIl (ad)	دراصل	in the real sense
dar'ar (a.m.s.)	دریٚر	strength
darun (v.m.s.)	درُن	to be stable *darIn'* (m.p.,f.s.) *darIni* (f.p.)
darga:h (m.)	درگاہ	a holy tomb, shrine
darjI (m.)	درجہٕ	class, place
darjan (a)	درجن	dozen
dardil (m.s.)	درٕدِل	sympathiser
darbIdar (ad)	دربدر	from pillar to post
darbIdAr' (n)	دربدری	wagabond
darba:r (m.s.)	دربار	office, court
darmIsha:stIr (m.)	درمہ شاستر	science of Dharma
darm'a:n (ad)	درمیان	in between
darma:rth (n)	درمارتھ	a religious trust
darya:v (m.)	دریاو	river
darIva:zI (m.)	درواز	door/doors
darshun (m.)	درشُن	glimpse
darvumIr (ad)	درعُمر	during the whole life
dastI (m.)	دستہ	diarrhoea
dasbastI (ad)	دس بستہ	handfolded
dava: (m.)	دوا	medicine
dava:t (f.s.)	دوات	inkpot *davA:ts* (p)
dava:kha:nI (m.)	دواخانہٕ	dispensary
dav dav (ad)	دَو دَو	race
davun (v.m.s.)	دوُن	to run *davIn'* (m.p.,f.s.) *davIni* (f.p.)
dasha:r (m.)	دشہار	Dussehra
dastiya:b (a)	دستیاب	available
dasta:r (m.)	دستار	turban
daha:n (m.)	دہان	mouth
da:h sanaska:r (m.)	داہ سنسکار	burning of the dead body
da:t (m.)	دات	metal
da:d (m.)	داد	thought, reality

da:d d'un (v)	داد دیُن	to praise
da:~d (m.)	دانٛد	ox, oxen, bull
da~:dIhavar (m.)	دانٛدِہوَر	yoke of oxen
da~:dur (m.s.)	دانٛدُر	vegetable seller, green grocer *da~:dar* (p)
da:n (m.)	دان	charity
da:n (m.)	دان	fire stove, hearth
da:nI (m.)	دانہٕ	grains/grain
da:ni	دانہِ	paddy
da:nikul (m.s.)	دانہِکُل	paddy plant *da:nikul'* (p)
da:na: (a.)	دانا	wise
da:nival (n)	دانہِوَل	corriander
da:n pa:tIr (m.)	دان پاتٕر	charity box
da:mnI (m.)	دامنہٕ	skirt, border
da:man (m.)	دامن	foot of a mountain
da:y (f.s.)	داے	maid servant, midwife *da:yi* (p)
da:r (m.s.)	دار	door, entrance of the house
da:r'al (m.s.)	دارِل	bearded person
da:run (v.m.s.)	دارُن	to owe *da:rIn'* (m.p.,f.s.) *da:rIni* (f.p.)
da:l (f.)	دال	pulses
da:la:n (m.)	دالان	balcony, verandah
da:lci:n (f.)	دالچِین	cinnamon
d'a:r (m.)	دیار	money, wealth
d'a:vun (vc.m.s.)	دیاوُن	to make someone give *d'a:vIn'* (m.p.,f.s.) *d'a:vIni* (f.p.)
dikath (f.s.)	دِقتھ	difficulty *diktI* (p)
digar (ad)	دِگر	about four o'clock in the evening
dil (m.)	دِل	heart
dilIvo:l (m.s.)	دِلہٕوول	courageous *dilIivA:l'* (p)
dila:sI (m.)	دِلاسہٕ	consolation
dilda:r (m.)	دِلدار	lover
dilkash (a)	دِلکش	attractive
divath (f.s.)	دِوَتھ	prestige
divgo:n (m.)	دِوگون	a ceremony of Hindu marriages
divA:li: (f.)	دِوالی	Dipawali - A Hindu festival
divta: (m.)	دِوتا	deity
divda:r (m.)	دِودار	deodar
di:gcI (m.)	دیگچہٕ	metal vessel, sauce pan
di:da:r (m.s.)	دیدار	glimpse
degul (m.)	دیگُل	an earthen pot
ded (f.s.)	دید	mother or grandmother
del (m.)	دیل	bark
dev (m.s.)	دیو	devil

devI (ad)	دیوِ	possibly, perhaps
de:va:nI (m.)	دیوانہٕ	mad
deva:nIgi: (f.s.)	دیوانہٕ گی	madness
de:g (f.s.)	دیگ	earthen vessel, large sauce pan *de:gI* (p)
de:li (m.)	دیلہِ	half paisa
de:vo:l (m.)	دیوول	insolvency
de:shbakhIti: (f.)	دیش بکھتی	patriotism
dukIr (f.s.)	دُکہٕر	twin *dukIri* (p)
dukA:r (f.s.)	دُکاٛر	scissors
duka:n (m.)	دُکان	shop(s)
duka:nda:r (m.)	دُکاندار	shopkeeper
dukhi: (m.)	دُکھی	worried, sad
duta:r (m.)	دُتار	a musical string instrument
d'un (vt.m.s.)	دِیُن	to give *din'* (m.p.,f.s.) *dini* (f.p.)
duniya: (m.s.)	دُنیاہ	world
duniyA:hi: (a)	دُنیاٛہی	worldly
dunamath (a)	دُنمتھ	ninety two
dupI (m.)	دُپہٕ	incence
dupa:se (pp)	دُپاسے	on both sides
duphA:r (m.)	دُپہر	noon
dub dub (ad)	دُب دُب	a pounding sound

dumda:m (nm.)	دُم دام	grand arrangement, pomp and show
durda:nI (m.)	دُردانہٕ	beautiful (a lover or a child)
duvanza:h (a)	دُونٛزاہ	fiftytwo
dushmanut (f.)	دُشمنتھ	enemity
dusI (m.)	دُسہٕ	fine woollen blanket
dusatath (a)	دُسٔتتھ	seventy two
duhA:Th (a)	دُہاٹھ	sixty-two
du:j (f.)	دوٗج	wooden slate *do:ji* (p)
du:t' (f.s.)	دوٗژ	saree *do:ti* (p)
du:n (m.)	دوٗن	carder *du:n'* (p)
du:n (a)	دوٗن	three-fourth
du:n' (f.)	دوٗنی	the burning fire used by Sadhus
du:r (m.)	دوٗر	ear ring(s)
du:r (ad)	دوٗر	far
du:r ande:sh (a)	دور اندیش	far-sighted, prudent
dogun (a)	دۆگُن	two fold
dph (m.)	دۆپھ	bush, thorn broom
dob (m.s.)	دۆب	washerman *dob'* (p)
dob' ba:y (f.s.)	دۆبی بایے	washer woman *dob' ba:yi* (p)
dobra:vun (v.m.s.)	دۆبراوُن	to bury *dobra:vIn'* (m.p.,f.s.) *dobra:vIni* (f.p.)

doyim (a)	دوٚیِم	second
dor (ad.m.s.)	دوٚر	hard *dAr'* (p) *dAr* (f.s.) *dari* (p)
dostu:r (m.)	دوٚستوٗر	custom
do:khI (m.)	دوکھ	deceit
do:zukh (m.)	دوزُکھ	hell
do:d (m.)	دود	disease
do:nun (vt.)	دونُن	carding (of cotton)
do:rI (m.)	دورِ	tour
do:run (v)	دورُن	to run
do:lath (m.)	دولتھ	wealth
do:s (m.)	دوس	friend
do:sti: (f.)	دوٚستی	friendship
dbIrun (vt.)	دوٚبرُن	to bury, hide in the ground
d>kh (m.)	دۄکھ	misery, sorrow
d>d (m.)	دۄد	milk
d>gIna:vun (vc.)	دۄگٕناوُن	to husk (grains), to pound
d>gIna:vun (vt.)	دۄگٕناوُن	to double
d>yitrIh (a)	دۄیتٕرٕہ	thirty two
d>yitA:ji: (a)	دۄیتاجی	forty two
d>yishi:th (a)	دۄیشیٹھ	eighty two
d>yun (vi.)	دۄیُن	to milk
d>shun (vi.)	دۄشُن	trickle
d>rlab (a.m.)	دۄرلب	difficult to find

d>la:b (m.)	دۄلاب	confusion
d>h (m.)	دۄہ	day
d>hdish (ad.)	دۄہدِش	daily
d>hay (ad)	دۄہَے	daily
d>h patI d>h (ad)	دۄہ پتہٕ دۄہ	day after day
d>h kh>tI d>h (ad)	دۄہ کھۄتہٕ دۄہ	day by day
d~:tshIra:vun (vt.)	دۄنٛژھراوُن	to scatter shabbily
drIy (f.)	دٕرۍ	oath
drA~:Thun (v.m.s.)	دٕرآنٛٹھُن	to plant *drA~:ThIn'* (m.p.,f.s.) *drA~:ThIni* (f.p.)
draThpA~:tsuk (m.)	دٕرٹھپانٛژک	pancak
dramun (m.)	دٕرمُن	a type of grass
dra:l (m.)	دٕرال	middleman, agent
drus (a.m.)	دٕرُس	correct
druy (m.s.)	دٕرۍ	husband's brother *drIy* (p.)
dre:Thun (vi.)	دٕراٹھُن	to harden
drog' (a.m.s.)	دٕروگ	expensive *drog'* (m.p.) *droj* (f.s.) *dr>ji* (f.p.)
drjar (f.s.)	دٕروجر	dearness
drgun (vi.)	دٕروگُن	to be dear, be expensive
drgIra:vun (vc.)	دٕروگراوُن	increase price
drkun (vi.)	دٕروکُن	to play, frisk

drkun (vi.m.s.)	دروکُن	to vomit
dro:t (m.s.)	دروٗت	sickle *drA:t'* (p)
drkh (f.s.)	دروکھ	vomitting *drkI* (p)

n

nI (ad)	نہٕ	not
nAkhrI (f.)	نخرٕ	mannerism
nAgIr (m.)	نگرٕ	city
nAzII (m.s.)	نزل	bad cold *nAzII sho:r* (m.)
nATin' (f.)	نٹِھنۍ	shivering
nAphi:s (a)	نفیس	nice
nAbi: (m.)	نبی	(Muslim) prophet
nAyim (a)	نیٔم	ninth
nAr (f.s.)	نرٕ	arm *nari* (p)
nAl'ci (f.)	نلیچہ	pipe of hubble-bubble
nAvi:d (m.)	نوید	prasad
nAs (a)	نس	a woman having small nose
nAsII (n)	نسل	breed
nAshi:lI (a)	نشیلہ	intoxicating
nAhA:r' (f.)	نہاری	breakfast
nAm'ra:vun (vt.)	نمراوُن	to make soft
nA:zir (m.)	ناظِر	revenue clerk
nA:yid (m.)	نآید	barber
nA:yib (m.)	نآیب	deputy, a revenue official
nA:r (f.s.)	نآر	water pot *na:ri* (p)
nA:rilI (m.)	نآریل	hubble-bubble
nA:pun (vi.)	نآپُن	to shine
na (ad)	نہ	no
nakId (m.)	نقد	cash
nakIb (m.)	نقب	house breaking
nakIvo:r (f.s.)	نکہ ووٗر	nostrill *nakIvA:r'* (p)
nakAlnavi:s (m.)	نقل نویس	copy writer
nakash nAvi:s (m.)	نقش نویس	draughtsman
naka:bI (m.)	نقابہ	veil
nakli: (a)	نقلی	artificial
nakh (m.)	نکھ	shoulder
nakhI (pp.)	نکھہ	close, near
nakhshi (m.)	نقشہٕ	map, design
nag (m.)	نگ	object, item
naga:rI (m.)	نگارہ	drum
nagmI (m.)	نغمہ	dance performance, melody
natsIna:vun (vc.m.s.)	نژناوُن	to make someone dance *natsIna:vIn'* (m.p.,f.s.) *natsIna:vIni* (f.p.)
natsun (v)	نژُن	to dance

natsan gor (m.s.)	نژن گوٗر	dancer *natsangAr'* (p) *natsangAr* (f.s.) *natsangari* (p)
nazra:nI (m.)	نذرانہٕ	present
nazar (m.)	نظر	glance
nazarband (m.)	نظربنٛد	detained
naza:kath (f.)	نزاکت	delicacy
naTun (v.m.s.)	نٔٹُن	to tremble, shiver *naTIn'* (m.p.,f.s.) *naTIni* (f.p.)
naTh (f.)	نٔٹھ	fear, shivering
naTIra:vun (vt.)	نٹہٕ راوُن	to cause to shiver
nethInon (a)	نٮ۪تھہٕ نوٗن	naked *nethInAn'* (m.p.,f.s.) *nethInani* (f.p.)
nadur (m.)	نٔدُر	lotus root *nadIr'* (p)
nada:math (a)	ندامتھ	humility
nada:rad (m.)	ندارد	nil
nanun (v.m.s.)	نَنُن	to be known, to come to light *nanIn'* (m.p.,f.s.) *nanIni* (f.p.)
napha: (m.)	نفع	profit
nab (m.)	نَب	sky
nabIdor (m.)	نبہٕ دوٗر	not raining, clear sky
nam (m.)	نَم	nail(s)
nam tsam ga:lIn' (vi)	نَم ژَم گالنۍ	to work very hard
namIra:vun (v)	نمہٕ راوُن	to make something bend
namIthim (a)	نمہٕ تھِم	ninetieth
namInamath (a)	نمہٕ نَمَتھ	ninety nine
namki:n (a)	نمکین	salty
namdI (m.)	نمدہٕ	felt carpet, rug
namath (a)	نَمَتھ	ninety
namaska:r (n)	نمسکار	greetings used by Hindus
namu:nI (m.)	نموٗنہٕ	sample
nambarda:r (m.)	نمبردار	village head man
nambal (m.)	نمبَل	marshy land
n'amun (v.m.s.)	نیٚمُن	to bow, to bend *n'amIn'* (m.p.,f.s.) *n'amIni* (f.p.)
namu:da:r (m.)	نموٗدار	appearance, appear
nay (f.s.)	نَے	flute, pipe, reed *nayi* (p)
nayshakar (m.)	نَے شکر	sugarcane
nar (m.)	نر	male
narIm (a)	نرم	soft
narImdil (a)	نرم دِل	kind hearted, mild
narkA:n'kul (m.s.)	نرکانۍ کُل	reed plant *narka:ni kul'* (p)
narukh (m.)	نرکھ	hell
nav (a)	نو	nine
navambar (m.)	نومبر	November
navisarI (ad)	نوِسرٕ	in a new way, wholly new

navun (vi.m.s.)	نوٗن	be excessive, to flourish *navIn'* (m.p.,f.s.) *navIni* (f.p.)
navun tI phlun (v)	نوٗن تہٕ پھلُن	to flourish
navreh (m.)	نوٗریٚہ	new year's day
nashI (m.)	نشہٕ	intoxication
nas (m.s.)	نٔس	nose *nasI* (p)
na:ka:mya:b (a)	ناکامیاب	unsuccessful, fail
na:ka:myA:bi: (f.s.)	ناکامیآبی	failure
na:g (m.)	ناگ	(water) spring
na:gIra:d (m.s.)	ناگٕراد	a small stream flowing from a spring
na:gIvo:n' (m.)	ناگہٕ وونۍ	spring water
na:gIhA:ni: (f.)	ناگہٕ ہانی	all of a sudden
na:c (m.)	ناچ	dance
na:ci:z (m.)	ناچیٖز	ordinary, insignificant
na:z (a)	ناز	pride
na:zni:n (m.)	نازنیٖن	delicate, beautiful, lovely
na:TI (f.)	ناٹہٕ	meat
na:Takh (m.)	ناٹکھ	drama, play
na:t (m.)	نعت	encomium, religious song of Muslims
na:da:n (a)	نادان	unwise, foolish

na:n' (f.)	نانۍ	grandmother
na:p (m.)	ناپ	measurement
na:pa:yAda:r (a)	ناپایدار	unstable, not durable
na:ph (f.)	ناف	navel
na:phI (m.)	نافہٕ	musk
na:phAham (a)	نافہم	immature, unwise
na:phalak (a)	نافلک	disobedient
na:bad (m.)	نابد	sugar candy
na:ma:va:r (a)	ناماوار	famous
na:mumkin (a)	ناممکن	impossible
n'a:y (m.)	نیاے	quarrel, dispute
na:r (m.)	نار	fire
na:rI (m.)	نعرٕ	slogan
na:rIji:l (m.)	نارٕجیٖل	coconut
na:rAng' (a)	نارنٛگۍ	tangerine orange
na:ri pista:n (m.)	ناری پِستان	breasts
na:l (m.)	نال	collar
na:lI (m.)	نالہٕ	rivulet
na:lA:n' (f.s.)	نالآنۍ	chappal, a footwear *na:la:ni* (p)
na:lun (v)	نالُن	to cry
na:val (m.)	ناوَل	novel
na:hvun (vt.)	ناہوُن	erase, to obliterate
na:vIsavA:r' (m.)	ناوٕ سوآرۍ	boating

n'a:vun (v.m.s.)	نیاوُن	to make someone take *n'a:vIn'* (m.p.,f.s.) *n'a:vIni* (f.p.)
na:v>me:d (a.)	ناوومید	frustrated
na:sa:z (a)	ناساز	bad, indisposed
na:stekh (m.)	ناستِک	athiest
nikI (m.)	نِکہٕ	baby boy
nic (f.s.)	نِچ	baby girl
nikamI (a)	نِکمہٕ	weak, lazy
nikun (vi.)	نِکُن	to become small
nikIra:vun (vt.)	نِکہٕ راوُن	to be cut into pieces
nic yaD (f.s.)	نِچ یڈ	lower part of belly
nib (f.s.)	نِب	nib
nilIvaTh (m.)	نِلہٕ وَٹھ	stone
niluc (m.)	نِلُچ	drake
nish (pp.)	نِش	near
niha:yat (a)	نہایت	very, much
ni:lam (m.)	نیٖلم	sapphire
necipAtir (f.s.)	نیچہٕ پَتُر	(Hindu) almanac
necuv (m.s.)	نیچوٕ	son *neciv'* (p)
nend (f.s.)	نیند	weeding paddy *nendI* (p)
nendIbA:th (m.)	نیندٕ باتھ	songs sung while weeding
nindIr (f.)	نیندٕر	sleep
nendur (m.s.)	نیندُر	a person who weeds (paddy) (weeder) *nendIr'* (p)

netun (vt.)	نیٚتُن	to shear (animals)
nemun (vi.)	نیٚمُن	to bow
nemIra:vun (vc.)	نیٚمہٕ راوُن	cause to bow, to bend
neni (f.)	نیٚنہٕ	mutton
nenibatI (m.)	نیٚنہٕ بتہٕ	meat and rice
neni mo~DIj (f.)	نیٚنہٕ مونڈُج	frog *nenimnDji* (p)
nenglun (vt.)	نیٚنگلُن	to swallow
nengIla:vun (v.m.s.)	نیٚنگہٕ لاوُن	to swallow *nengIla:vIn'* (m.p.,f.s.) *nengIla:vIni* (f.p.)
nebar (ad)	نیٚبَر	outside
nema:z (f.)	نیٚماز	(Muslim) prayer
nerakh (m.)	نیٚرخ	rate,price
nerakhna:mI (m.)	نیٚرخ نامہٕ	price list
nera:sh (f.)	نیٚراش	disappointed
nera:ha:r (m.)	نیٚراہار	complete fast
neshIbod (a)	نیٚشہٕ بوٚد	innocent
ne:kh (a)	نیکھ	good, noble
ne:zI (m.s.)	نیزٕ	lance, spear
ne:thIr (m.)	نیتھٕر	marriage
ne:b (m.)	نیب	address, clue
ne:run (vi.m.s.)	نیرُن	to depart, start, go forth *ne:rIn'* (m.p.,f.s.) *ne:rIni* (f.p.)
ne:shun (v)	نیشُن	to appreciate

n'uk (a.m.s.)	نۄک	small *nik'* (p)
n'uk n'uk (ad)	نۄک نۄک	very little, small pieces
n'uk de:lI (m.)	نۄک دیلہٕ	small penny
n'un (v.m.s.)	نِیُن	to take *nin'* (m.p.,f.s.) *nini* (f.p.)
numA:yish (f.)	نُمائش	exhibition
nu:n (m.)	نوٗن	salt
nu:nIda:r (a)	نوٗنہٕ دار	salted
nu:r (m.)	نوٗر	brilliance
nu:rImot (a.m.s.)	نوٗرٕموت	graceful
n'u:l (a.m.s.)	نیوٗل	green, blue, raw *ni:l'* (p) *ni:j* (f.s.) *ni:ji* (p)
ni:lun (vi.)	نیٖلُن	greening, become blue, green
nu:l (m.)	نوٗل	mangoose
n'u:l k'om (m.)	نیوٗل کیوم	caterpiller *ni:l' kem'* (p)
nokus (m.)	نۄقص	drawback
noT (m.)	نۄٹ	earthen pitcher *nAT'* (p)
n'oTh (m.s.)	نیوٹھ	thumb
non tI chon (a)	نۄن تہٕ چھۄن	very poor
n'om (m.s.)	نیوم	lemon *nem'* (p)
n'un (vt.)	نِیُن	to take
n'a:vun (vc.)	نیاوُن	cause to take
nomra:vun (v.m.s.)	نۄمراوُن	to bend, to make soft nomIra:vIn' (m.p.,f.s.) nomIra:vIni (f.p.)
nomu:nI (m.)	نۄموٗنہٕ	sample
novra:vun (vt.)	نۄوراوُن	make excessive
nor (m.s.)	نۄر	sleeve *nAr'* (p)
nophul (m.)	نۄفُل	a Muslim prayer for rain
nol (m.s)	نۄل	tube *nAl'* (p)
nov (a.m.s.)	نۄو	new *nAv'* (p) *nAv* (f.s.) *navi* (p)
nov rakh (m.)	نۄو رخ	new dress
nos (a)	نۄس	a man with small nose, pugnosed ادلس
no:kar (m.)	نوکر	servant
no:kh (m.)	نوکھ	point
no:zukh (a)	نوزُکھ	delicate
no:Th (m.)	نوٹھ	note (rupees)
n>kus (m.)	نٲقص	defect
n>khtI (m.)	نُکتہٕ	point
n>khsa:n (m.)	نُقصان	loss
n>sh (f.s.)	نۄش	daughter-in-law *n>shI* (p)

p

pI~tsIh (a)	پنٛژٕہ	twenty five

pI~:tsim (a) پینٛژِم fifth

pAchin (f.s.) پٔچھِن fowl

pAj (f.s.) پٔج a basket
paji (p)

pA~z (f.s.) پٔنٛز monkey
pa~zI (p)

pAz' kin' (ad) پٔزِ کِنۍ really, in fact

pAz'yo:r (a) پٔزیور a person who speaks truth

pAz' pA:Th' (ad) پٔزِ پٲٹھۍ truly, actually, really

pAT (f.s.) پٔٹ plank of wood
paci (p)

pAt' (ad) پٔتۍ at the back side

pAd' (m.p.) پٔدۍ foot steps

pArista:n (m.s.) پٔرِستان a place where fairies live

pAri: (f.s.) پٔری fairy
pAriyi (p)

pAri:kh'a: (f.) پٔریکھیا test

pAt' bru~:Th' (ad) پٔتۍ بروٗنٛٹھۍ from all sides

pAtshil (f.s.) پٔژھِل a pre-marriage ceremony in Muslims

pAs' (f.s.) پٔسۍ landslide
pasi (p)

pAsi:nI (m.) پٔسیٖنہٕ sweat

pA:tsh'palav (n) پٲژھۍ پلو a dress for special occasions

pA:ja:mI (m.) پٲجامہٕ payjama, trousers

pA:z (m.) پٲز hawk, falcon

pA:n' pa:nay (pr) پانٛنۍ پانَے of its own

pA:T' gots (f.) پٲٹۍ گوژ silk cocoon

pA:T' pan (m.) پٲٹۍ پَن silken thread

pata:h (f.) پتاہ address, whereabouts

path kun (ad) پَتہٕ کُن backwards, behind

pangath (f.) پَنٛگتھ crowd

pA:r (f.) پٲرہ hut

pA:ravka:r (n) پٲروکار follower

pA:lish (f.) پالِش polish

pA~:sI (m.) پٲنٛسہٕ money, coins

pakIna:vun (v.m.s.) پَکہٕ ناوُن to cause to walk
pakIna:vIn' (m.p.,f.s.)
pakIna:vIni (f.p.)

pakun (v) پَکُن to walk

pako:ri (f.) پکوٗرِ fried vegetable snacks

pakh (m.s.) پکھ wing
pakhI (p)

pa~khI (m.) پنٛکھہٕ fan, fans

paga:h (ad) پگاہ tomorrow

pach (ad) پَچھ fortnight

pachim (m.) پَچھِم west

pachta:vun (vi.) پَچھتاوُن to regret

pacha:nun (vt.) پَچھانُن to recognize

patsh (f.) پَژھ belief

patsun (v.m.s.)	پَژُن	to trust (with a loan) *patsIn'* (m.p.,f.s.) *patsIni* (f.p.)
pazi manI (m.)	پزِ منہٕ	with sincerity
p'aTh (p.p.)	پٮ۪ٹھ	on, upon
p'aThI (p.p.)	پٮ۪ٹھہٕ	from
paThvA:r' (m.)	پٹھوٲرۍ	a revenue official
paDA:y (f.)	پڑاے	studies
paDur (m.s.)	پڑُر	hoof *paDar* (p)
patI (ad)	پَتہٕ	afterwards
patIlu:n (m.)	پتلوٗن	pants
patangI (m.)	پتنگہٕ	kite/kites
patavla:kan (ad)	پتوٚلاکن	lastly, after all
path ka:li (ad)	پتھ کالہِ	in the past
pathkun (ad)	پتھکُن	backwards
pan (m.)	پَن	leaves
pan (m.)	پَن	thread
panIpo~:pur (m.s.)	پنہٕ پوٚنپُر	butterfly *panIpo~:par* (p)
panIvAthIr (m.)	پنہٕ وُتھر	leaf,leaves
panc (m.)	پنٛچ	panchayat member
panca:yat (m.)	پنچایت	panchayat
pantsa:h (a)	پنژاہ	fifty
pantsA:him (a)	پنژٲہِم	fiftieth
panjI (m.)	پنجہٕ	paw, claw
panjIrI (m.)	پنجرہٕ	cage
panjA:b' ( )	پنجٲبۍ	Punjabi

panda:h (a)	پنٛداہ	fifteen
papun (v.m.s.)	پَپُن	to ripen *papIn'* (m.p.,f.s.) *papIni* (f.p.)
pampo:sh (m.)	پمپوش	lotus flower
pambuch (m.)	پمبچھ	lotus seed
pay (m.)	پے	address, whereabouts
payun (v.m.s.)	پیُن	to bake *payin'* (m.p.,f.s.) *payini* (f.p.)
payga:m (m.)	پیغام	message
paylaT (m.)	پیلٹ	pilot
par (m.)	پر	big hammar
parkha:vun (v.m.s.)	پرکھاوُن	to test *parkha:vIn'* (m.p.,f.s.) *parkha:vIni* (f.p.)
parIna:vun (v.m.s.)	پرناوُن	to teach *parIna:vIn'* (m.p.,f.s.) *parIna:vIni* (f.p.)
parvardiga:r (m.)	پروردگار	God
parIva:y (m.)	پرواے	care, concern
par'un (m.s.)	پرٕیُن	sieve *parin'* (p)
parun (v.m.s.)	پرُن	to read *parIn'* (m.p.f.s.) *parIni* (f.p.)
parganI (m.)	پرگنہٕ	province, subdivision
parcu:n (m.)	پرچوٗن	retail

pardI (m.)	پردٕ	curtain, curtains
parma:tma: (m.)	پرماتما	almighty, God
parma:nI (m.)	پرمانہٕ	weights & measures
parmi:shar (m.)	پرمیشور	God almighty
parastish (m.)	پرستِش	worship
parus (ad)	پرُس	last year
parhe:z (n)	پرہیز	abstinence
parhe:zga:r (a)	پرہیزگار	one who observes abstinence
parkha:vun (vt.)	پرکھاوُن	to test
pal (m.)	پل	moment
pal (m.)	پل	rock,.boulder
palangI (m.)	پلنگہٕ	wooden bed
palav (m.)	پلَو	clothes
palzun (vi.)	پلزُن	be useful, come to help
palTun (vi.)	پلٹُن	damp
pavI (m.)	پوٕ	quarter of wine (1/4 of a bottle)
pash (m.)	پش	roof
pashun (v)	پشُن	to repent
pashe:ma:n (m.)	پشیمان	remorseful, be sorry
pashpun (v.m.s.)	پشپُن	to drip (drop by drop), leak *pashpIn'* (m.p.,f.s.) *pashpIni* (f.p.)
pas (m.s.)	پس	pus

pazun (vi.)	پزُن	turn out to be true
pazIra:vun (vi.)	پزراوُن	prone to be true
parcI (m.)	پرچہٕ	piece of paper, question paper
pa:h (m.)	پاہ	manure
paha:D (m.)	پہاڑ	mountain
pa:gal (a)	پاگل	mad
pa:zun (vi.m.s.)	پازُن	to bring out from, to cleanse *pa:zIn'* (m.p.,f.s.) *pa:zIni* (f.p.)
pa:thun (vi.)	پاتھُن	be available
pa:paD (n)	پاپڑ	papad
p̂:kIna:vun (v̂c.)	پاکہٕناوُن	to boil, to cook
p'a:lI (m.)	پیالہٕ	cup
p'a:v (m.)	پیاو	parents' presents to the mother of a newly born baby
pa~:zu: (m.)	پانٛزوٗ	about two and half kilograms
pa~:tsItrIh (a)	پانٛژترٕہ	thirty five
pa~:tsItA:ji (a)	پانٛژتاجی	forty five
pa~:tsInamath (a)	پانٛژنمتھ	ninety five
pa~:tsIvanza:h (a)	پانٛژونزاہ	fifty five
pa~:tsIshi:th (a)	پانٛژشیٹھ	eighty five

pa~:tsIsatath (a)	پانژٕستتھ	seventy five
pa~:tsIhA:Th (a)	پانژٕہاٹھ	sixty five
pa:kh (m.)	پاکھ	pus, boiling
pa:kh (a)	پاکھ	pure
pa~:gADvI (m.)	پان گڈوٕ	pot full of water
pa~:tsh (a)	پانژھ	five
pa:Th (m.)	پاٹھ	holy verses/hymns
pa:Thsha:la: (f.)	پاٹھشالا	school for children
pa:dIr' (m.)	پادٕر	priest of a church.
pa:n (m.)	پان	beetle leaves
pa:n (pr.)	پان	self
pa:nIvA:n' (pr.)	پانٕہ وٲنۍ	among one another, mutually
pa~:n'ur (m.)	پانٛیُر	water man
pa:parja: (a)	پاپرجا	prosperous
pa:ph (m.)	پاپھ	sin, sins, blemish
pa:y (n)	پاے	alternative, way out
pa:yIda:r (a)	پایہٕ دار	static, strong, lasting
pa:rak (f.)	پارک	park
pa:rud (m.)	پارُد	mercury
pa:rTi: (f.)	پارٹی	party
pa:lakh (f.)	پالکھ	spinnach
pa:lun (v.m.s.)	پالُن	to bring up, to feed, to protect *pa:lIn'* (m.p.,f.s.) *pa:lIni* (f.p.)
pa:lsi: (f.)	پالسی	policy
pa:v (f.)	پاو	one fourth of a seer
pa:vun (v.m.s.)	پاوُن	to let fall *pa:vIn'* (m.p.,f.s.) *pa:vIni* (f.p.)
pa:run (vt.)	پارُن	to plait the hair
pa:s (m.)	پاس	pass
pa:sI (m.)	پاسہٕ	pure (gold)
piTun (v.m.s.)	پِٹُن	to be beaten up, to be forced to wait *piTIn'* (m.p.,f.s.) *piTIni* (f.p.)
piTIna:vun (v.m.s.)	پِٹہٕ ناوُن	to make somebody to wait *piTIna:vIn'* (m.p.,f.s.) *piTIna:vIni* (f.p.)
pitur (m.s.)	پِتُر	cousin *pitIr'* (m.p.)
pitra:th	پِتراتھ	enemity among cousins
pith (f.s.)	پِتھ	a kind of (skin) disease
pilIna:vun (v.m.s.)	پِلہٕ ناوُن	to handover, to reach *pilIna:vIn'* (m.p.,f.s.) *pilIna:vIni* (f.p.)
pilun (vi.m.s.)	پِلُن	be possible, reach *pilIn'* (m.p.,f.s.) *pilIni* (f.p.)
pishlun (vi.)	پِشلُن	be soft, become slippery
pisto:l (m.)	پستول	pistol

pihun (v.m.s.)	پِہُن	to grind *pihIn'* (m.p.,f.s.) *pihIni* (f.p.)
piTun (vi.)	پِٹُن	wait wearily
piThIra:vun (vc.)	پِٹھٕراوُن	to blame, to criticise
pi:n (m.)	پیٖن	delivery
pi:r (f.)	پیٖر	generation
pi:r (m)	پیٖر	Muslim priest
pi:rImarId (m.)	پیٖرٕ مرٕد	old man
pi:shin (ad)	پیٖشِن	afternoon
pi:shi: (m.p.)	پیٖشی	attendance in a court
pecan' (f.s.)	پیچھنۍ	aunt (father's brother's wife) *pecIni* (p)
peTro:l (m.)	پیٹرول	petrol
petIr (m.)	پیتٕر	uncle (father's brother)
petIra:vun (vc.)	پیتٕراوُن	to bear the brunt
pensal (m.)	پینسل	pencil
pevun (v.m.)	پیوُن	to lit the oven
pe:n lagIn' (v)	پیٖن لگٕنۍ	to be sharpened
pe:Ti (f.p)	پیٖٹہِ	packing boxes
pe:parmA:shi: (f.)	پیٖپرماشی	papier machie
pe:shI (m.)	پیٖشہٕ	occupation, profession
pe:sh laphIz (m.)	پیٖش لفظ	preface
puj (m.)	پُج	butcher
puj'ba:y (f.s.)	پُج بایہ	butcher's wife
puThI (a)	پُٹھہٕ	opposite, odd
punar zanIm (m.)	پُنر زنٕم	rebirth
punun (vi.)	پُنُن	to come true, affect (a curse)
punim (f.)	پُنِم	purnamashi (the 15th moon)
puran (f.)	پُرن	a piece of land for house
pur kholu:s (a)	پُر خلوص	sincere
putsun/ putsra:vun (vt.)	پُژُن / پُژراوُن	to cut (grass, flowers etc.) into pieces
pushI (ad)	پُشہٕ	extra
pushIra:vun (v.m.s.)	پُشٕراوُن	to handover, force to take *pushIra:vIn'* (m.p.,f.s.) *pushIra:vIni* (f.p.)
pursoku:n (a)	پُرسکوٗن	peaceful
pulsIvo:l (m.)	پُلسہٕ وول	policeman *pulsIvA:l'* (p)
pulho:r (m.)	پُلہور	shoes made of grass ropes *pulhA:r'* (p)
puhur (m.)	پُہُر	a kind of snake
pu:ts (f.)	پوٗژ	headgear used by old Hindu women
puThIra:vun (v.m.s.)	پُٹھٕراوُن	to wash, to clean *puThIra:vIn'* (m.p.,f.s.) *puThIra:vIni* (f.p.)
pu:t' (m.p.)	پوٗتۍ	chicken, chicks

pu:nvI (f.)	پۄنوٕ	cracks in feet
pu:r (m.)	پوٗر	east
pu:r' (f.)	پوٗرِ	Puri - wheat puffs
pu:run (vi.)	پوٗرُن	to last
pu:zun (vt.)	پوٗزُن	to worship
pu:rIpA:Th' (ad)	پوٗرٕ پاٹھۍ	fully, very well, completely
pokhAr (m.)	پۄکھر	pond
potsh (m.s.)	پۄژھ	guest *pAtsh'* (p)
pAtsh'lo:v (m.s.)	پٔژھلوو	fox *pAtshlA:v'* (p)
po~z (m.s.)	پۄنٛز	monkey *pA~z'* (p)
poTh (a)	پۄٹھ	strong
pot (ad)	پۄت	backwards
p'ot (m.s.)	پیۄت	nib, tip *pet'* (p)
p'ush (m.s)	پیُش	flea *pish (p)*
potul (m.)	پوتُل	idol
potmanzar (m.)	پوت منظر	background
pon' (m.)	پونۍ	good deeds
p'on (v.m.s.)	پیۄن	to fall *pen'* (m.p.,f.s.) *peni* (f.p.)
pop (a.m.s.)	پۄپ	ripe *pAp'* (p) *pAp* (a.f.s.) *papi* (f.p.)
poru:zanIm (m.)	پوٗروٗزَنم	previous birth
pormut l'u:khumut (a.m.s.)	پۄرمُت لیوٗکھمُت	literate (person) *pAr'mIt' li:khmIt'* (p) *pArmIts li:chmIts* (a.f.s.) *parimatsI le:chmatsI* (p)
pol (a)	پۄل	thin, weak
pola:v (m.)	پۄلاو	fried rice, Pilau
posh (m.)	پۄش	animal
poh (m.)	پوہ	Posh - name of a month of Bikram era
pohal (m.)	پۄہل	shepherd
p'ol (m.s.)	پیۄل	testicle *pel'* (p)
pokhtI (a)	پوختہٕ	firm, ripe
po:g (m.)	پوگ	horn
po:char (m.)	پوچھر	strength, strong, improvement
po:tsh (m.s.)	پوژھ	inner cotton pheran *pA:tsh'* (p)
po:ThIra:vun (v.m.s.)	پوٹھراوُن	to clean (hands) to clean fish *po:ThIra:vIn'* (m.p.,f.s.) *po:ThIra:vIni* (f.p.)
po:Dar (m.)	پوڈر	powder
po:tur (m.)	پوتُر	pan of a scale
po:n' (m.)	پونۍ	water
po:run (v.m.s.)	پورُن	to overcome, to affect *po:rIn'* (m.p.,f.s.) *po:rIni* (f.p.)
po:v (m.s.)	پوو	lung of the ladder, one step *pA:v'* (p)

po:r (m.)	پور	storey
po:sh (m.s.)	پوش	flower
po:shIgond (m.)	پوشہٕ گونٛڈ	bouque, bunch of flowers
po:shIcaman (m.)	پوشہٕ چَمَن	flower bed
po:shIpu:za: (f.)	پوشہٕ پوٗزا	flower ceremony in Hindu marriage
po:shI thAr (f.s.)	پوشہٕ ٹھٔر	flower bush, flower plant *po:shI thari* (p)
po:shI d>ph (m.)	پوشہٕ دوپھ	flower bush *po:shI vA:r* (p)
po:shIvun (a.m.s.)	پوشہٕ وُن	everlasting *po:shIvIn'* (a.f.s.)
po:shun (v.m.s.)	پوشُن	to last, be victorious *po:shIn'* (m.p.,f.s.) *po:shIni* (f.p.)
p>khtI (ad)	پوخٕتہٕ	ripe, metalled
p>ph (f.s.)	پوپھ	father's sister *p>phI* (p)
p>phuv (m.s.)	پوپھو	father's sister's husband p>phIv' (p)
prItshIna:vun (vc.m.s.)	پٕرٕژھناوُن	to ask *prItshIna:vIn'* (m.p.,f.s.) *prItshIna:vIni* (f.p.)
prItshun (v.m.s.)	پٕرٕژھُن	to ask *prItshIn'* (m.p.,f.s.) *prItshIni* (f.p.)
prInsipal (m.s.)	پرٕنسپل	principal
prakhTun (vi.)	پرٔکھٹُن	be manifest, to appear
praka:sh (m.)	پرٛکاش	light
pratsh (f.)	پرٛژھ	riddle *pratshI* (p)
praza: (f.)	پرٛزا	subject, the governed, the ruled
prath ka~:h (a.)	پرٛتھ کانٛہہ	everyone
prath tAri:kI (ad)	پرٛتھ طریقہٕ	in every way
prath tarIphI (ad)	پرٛتھ طرفہٕ	on each side
prath doh (ad)	پرٛتھ دوہ	everyday
prath vizi (ad)	پرٛتھ وِزِ	every time
prang (m.)	پرٛنٛگ	tomb
praba:th (m.)	پرٛباتھ	dawn
prama:n (m.)	پرٛمان	evidence, proof
pralay (m.)	پرٛلے	deluge
prasun (v.m.s)	پرٛسُن	to give birth *prasIn'* (m.p.,f.s.) prasIni (f.p.)
prazIna:vun (vt.)	پرٛزناوُن	to recognize
prazlun (vi.)	پرٛزلُن	to shine
pranun (vi.)	پرٛنُن	to become white, to be clean
prayun (vi.)	پرٛیُن	be pleased with, to like
pra:ga:sh (m.)	پرٛاگاش	sunshine
pra:ts (f.)	پرٛاژ	corner of mouth
pra:Tun (vt.)	پرٛاٹُن	to dig

pra:nIva:r (m.)	پرانہٕ وار	used clothes, old garment
pra:nIharIsh (a)	پرانہٕ ہرش	terrified, be shaken
pra:ta:ka:l (ad.)	پراتاکال	day break, early morning
pra:n (m.)	پران	soul
pra:n (m.)	پران	garlic
pra:run (v.m.s.)	پرارُن	to wait, waiting *pra:rIn'* (m.p.,f.s.) *pra:rIni* (f.p.)
pra:rthana: (f.)	پرارتھنا	prayer
pra:lab (m.)	پرالب	luck, fate, destiny
pra:vun (v.m.s.)	پراوُن	to get, to achieve *pra:vIn'* (m.p.,f.s.) *pra:vIni* (f.p.)
pra:nun (vi.)	پرانُن	become old
pra:h (m.)	پراہ	an abuse
prazi:DanT (m.)	پرزیڈنٹ	president
prA:p'un (m.)	پرایپُن	a ritual in Hindu worship for sanctifying edible to perform this ritual *prA:p' un ha:vun* (vi.)
pron (a.m.s.)	پرۆن	fair complexioned *prAn'* (m.p.,f.s.) *preni* (f.p.)
pro:n (a.m.s.)	پرون	old, worn out *prA:n'* (m.p.,f.s.) *pra:ni* (f.p.)

ph

phAki:r (m.)	فقیر	beggar
phAtilI (m.)	پھٹِلہٕ	wick like amulet made of paper
phAr (f.)	پھٔر	dried fish
phArith gatshun (v)	پھٔرِتھ گژھُن	to steal
phArya:d (m.)	فریاد	plaint
phAr'yA:d' gatshun (v)	فریادی گژھُن	to make a plaint
phAl' (m.p.)	پھٔلی	pieces
phAl'lI (m.)	پھٔلِلہٕ	scent
phAl'sItsan (f.s.)	پھٔلہٕ سِژن	paper pin
phA:tir (a)	پھاتر	mad
phA:tirA:zi: (f.)	پھاترِ آزی	madness
phA:shIn (m.)	فیشن	fashion
phA~:s' (f.)	پھانٔسی	strangulation, hanging-capital punishment
phakath (ad)	فقط	only
phakIlad (a)	پھکہٕ لد	full of stench, stink
phakh (a)	پھکھ	bad smell, stench
phakhIr (m.)	فخر	pride, glory
phazIl (m.)	فضل	kindness, grace, mercy
phaTIva~:gun (m.)	پھٹہٕ وانگُن	a budding brinjal, an abuse
phaTa:phaT (ad)	پھٹاپھٹ	at once, immediately

phaTun (v.m.s.)	پھٹُن	to drown/sink, be split *phaTIn'* (m.p.,f.s.) *phaTIni* (f.p.)
pha~D (m.)	فنڈ	fund
phabun (vi.)	پھبُن	be excellent, to progress
phatrath (f.)	پھترٕتھ	muisance
phata:h (m.)	فتح	victory
pha~d (m.)	پھند	deceit
pha~dba:z (a)	پھندباز	cunning, deceitful
phan (m.)	فن	art
phana:h (v)	فناہ	extinguish, ruin
phanka:r (m.)	فن کار	artist, musician
phangI (a)	پھنگٕ	loafer
phanDIr (f.)	پھنڈٕر	youthful lady, robust lady
phamb (m.)	پھمب	cotton
phambIva:l (m.)	پھمبٕ وال	a hair of cotton
phamva:r (m.)	پھنوار	fountain
phaya:z (a)	فیاض	generous
pharIma:vun (v.m.s.)	فرماوُن	to order, command *pharma:vIn'* (m.p.,f.s.) *pharma:vIni* (f.p.)
pharakh (f.)	فرق	difference
ph'aran (m.)	پھہرن	Kashmiri loose dress, overalls
phara:gath (f.)	فراگتھ	leisure, relief

pharun (v.m.s.)	پھُرن	to steal *pharIn'* (m.p.,f.s.) *pharIni* (f.p.)
pharo:g (m.)	فروگ	encouragement
pharo:g d'un (vt. m.s)	فروگ دیُن	to encourage, prosper
phardI (m.)	فردٕ	piece, sheet
pharma:n (n)	فرمان	order, edict
pharma:barda:r (a.)	فرمانبردار	obedient
pharvari: (f.)	فروری	February
pharla~:g (m.)	فرلانگ	furlong
phalun (vi.)	پھلُن	wear away, become old (of clothes), bear fruit
phal (m.)	پھل	fruit/fruits
phala:n (m.)	فلان	penis
phalvA:y (a)	پھلوآے	mad
phasIl (m.)	فصل	crop
phasIra:vun (vt.)	پھسراوُن	to entrap (someone)
phalha:r (m.)	پھل ہار	food consisting of fruit only, pudding
phasun (vi.)	پھسُن	be entrapped, caught
phasun (v.m.s.)	پھسُن	to be involved *phasIn'* (m.p.,f.s.) *phasIni* (f.p.)
phasa:vun (v.m.s.)	پھساوُن	to involve (someone)
pha:kI (m.)	فاقٕ	fast (kept by Hindus)

pha:gun (m.)	پھاگُن	Phagun - name of the eleventh month of Bikram era
pha~:gun (vi.)	پھانٛگُن	cry (of cuts), mew
pha~:phlun (vi.)	پھانٛپھلُن	be prosperous, develop physically
pha:Takh (m.)	پھاٹکھ	house for stray cattle
pha:Takh (m.)	پھاٹک	gate
pha:teh (m.)	فاتِح	prayer for dead
pha:ram (m.)	فارم	farm
pha:l (m.)	پھال	ploughshare
pha:lun (v.m.s.)	پھالُن	to cut to pieces, split (wood) *pha:lIn'* (m.p.,f.s.) *pha:lIni* (f.p.)
pha:ltu: (ad)	فالتوٗ	extra
phiza: (m.)	فِضا	scene, bloom
phida: (a)	فِدا	sacrifice, devoted (to)
phitnI (m.)	فِتنہٕ	trouble, mischief
phira:kh (m.s.)	پھِراکھ	frock
phirith (n)	پھِرِتھ	reversed
phirkI (m.)	فِرقہٕ	community
phirkIparast (m.)	فِرقہٕ پرست	communal, prejudicial
phirIna:vun (v.m.s.)	پھِرٕناوُن	to move something *phirIna:vIn'* (m.p.,f.s.) *phirIna:vIni* (f.p.)
phirun (vt.)	پھِرُن	turn over (pages), pour from one vessel to another *phirIn'* (m.p.,f.s.) *phirIni* (f.p.)
phirIsa:l (m.)	پھِرٕسال	first visit of groom to inlaws after marriage
phirIthur (m.)	پھِرٕتھُر	change of place (during a Hindu marriage)
phirdo:s (m.)	فِردوس	paradise
phiri:ni: (n)	پھِرینی	sweet pudding
phil pho:r (ad)	فِل فور	at once
philim (m.)	فِلِم	film
phis (f.s.)	پھِس	penis (of a boy)
phi:kI (a)	پھیکہٕ	fade
phi:tI (m.)	فیتہٕ	lace
phel (m.)	پھیل	a boil
phe:rIvun (m.s.)	پھیرٕوُن	wandering man *phe:rIvIn'* (m.p.,f.s.) *phe:rIvIni* (f.p.)
phe:run (v.m.s.)	پھیرُن	to roam about *phe:rIn'* (m.p.,f.s.) *phe:rIni* (f.p.)
phe:run (vi.)	پھیرُن	to miss someone
phe:l (v)	فیل	fail
phe:shun (v.m.s.)	پھیشُن	to lick *phe:shIn'* (m.p.,f.s.) *phe:shIni* (f.p.)
phi:s (m.)	فیس	fee
phe:rIvo:l (m.)	پھیرٕوول	hawker *phe:rIvA:l'* (p)

phuTvo:T (m.)	پھٹ ووٹ	change, small coins
phuTIra:vun (v.m.s.)	پھٹھراوُن	to break *phuTIra:vIn'* (m.p.,f.s.) *phuTIra:vIni* (f.p.)
phuTun (vi.)	پھٹُن	be broken
phuTba:l (f.)	فُٹ بال	football
phul (m.)	پھُل	baking soda
phuhIr (f.)	پھُہر	burnt rice
phukun (vi.)	پھُکُن	to blow a fire (with the mouth)
phu:T (f.)	پھوٗٹ	dispute
phu:l(go:bi:) (m.)	پھوٗل (گوبی)	cauliflower
ph'ok (m.s.)	پھیوٚک	shoulder *phek'* (p)
phot (m.)	پھوٚت	basket
phoph (a.m.s.)	پھوٚپھ	a stammerer *phAph'* (p) *phAph* (f.s.) *phaphi* (p)
phozu:l (m.)	فضوٗل	useless
ph'or (m.)	پھیوٚر	drop
ph'a:run (vi.)	پھیارُن	rinse, to take out water
pholu:dI (n)	پھولوٗدٕ	porridge
pho:j (m.)	فوج	army
pho:ran (ad)	فورن	at once
pho:run (vi.)	پھورُن	quiver, flutter
pho:la:d (m.)	فولاد	steel
phkh (n)	پھوکھ	blow
phtIr (f.)	پھوتر	a kind of basket *phtIri* (p)
ph>lun (vi.m.s.)	پھوٚلُن	to bloom *ph>lIn'* (m.p.,f.s.) *ph>lIni* (f.p.)
phlIra:vun (v.m.s.)	پھولہٕ راوُن	to blossom *phlIra:vIn'* (m.p.,f.s.) *phlIra:vIni* (f.p.)
ph>shun (v)	پھوشُن	to be angry
phrakun (vi.)	پھرکُن	panting, be out of breath
phrakh (m.)	پھرکھ	sigh, breath
phras (m.)	پھرس	poplar tree

b

bI (pr)	بہٕ	I
bA~gIr (f.s.)	بٔنگر	bangle *bA~grI* (p)
bAcra:vun (v.m.s.)	بچھراوُن	to save, to lay by *bAcra:vIn'* (m.p.,f.s.) *bAcra:vIni* (f.p.)
bATvI (m.)	بٹوٕ	money bag, purse
bAnith yun (v)	بنتھ یُن	to fall on bad days, to meet bad luck
bAnglI (m.)	بنگلہٕ	bunglow
bAndish (f.)	بندش	restriction
bAn'ya:n (f.s.)	بنیان	sweater *bAn'ya:nI* (p)

bAt' (f.s.)	بٔتؠ	tin lamp
bAdi: (f.s.)	بٔدی	malice, wickedness
bAr (f.s.)	بٔر	a chink
bArIts (a.f.s.)	بٔرٕژ	pregnant *bArItsI* (p)
bArith (a)	بٔرِتھ	full
bAyka:kan' (f.s.)	بٔیکاکٔنؠ	brother's wife *bAyka:kni* (p)
bAl' (ad)	بٔلؠ	without any aim, casually
bAlki (c)	بلکہ	but, moreover
bAsti: (f.)	بستی	population, settlement
bAlIra:vun (vt.)	بٔلٕراوُن	to cure
bAhrI (m.)	بٔہرٕ	waiter
bAhas (m.s.)	بحث	discussion
bAhA:la:vun (v.m.s.)	بٔہلاوُن	to recreate, to amuse *bAhA:la:vIn'* (m.p.,f.s.) *bAhA:la:vIni* (f.p.)
bAhi: (f.)	بہی	account-book, ledger, day book
bAhi:kha:tI (m.s.)	بہی کھاتہٕ	ledger
bA:g (m.s.)	بآگ	bag
bA:g' (ad)	بآگؠ	near about
bA:gIra:vun (v.m.s.)	بآگٕراوُن	to distribute *bA:gIra:vIn'* (m.p.,f.s.) *bA:gIra:vIni* (f.p.)

bA:gIrun (v.m.s.)	بآگٕرُن	to distribute *bA:gIrIn'* (m.p.,f.s.) *bA:gIrIni* (f.p.)
bA:ts (m.)	بآژ	family member, spouse
bA:z' (f.s.)	بآزؠ	deceit
bA:z'gar (m.)	بآزیگر	juggler
bA:Th (m.)	بآٹھ	bat
bA:th (m.)	بآتھ	song
bA:dIr (m.)	بآدٕر	Bahdun - name of the fifth month fo Bikrami era
bA:rav (n)	بآرَو	deity, shiva
bA:risTar (m.)	بآرِسٹر	barrister
bA:r' thaph (f.)	بآرؠ ٹھپھ	hand-ful of mud
bA:y band (m.)	بآے بنٛد	relations
bA:skal (m.)	بآیسکل	bicycle
bakhIt (m.)	بخت	luck
bakhti: (ad)	بھکتی	devotion
bakhshun (v.m.s.)	بخشُن	to forgive, to present a gift *bakhshIn'* (m.p.,f.s.) *bakhshIni* (f.p.)
bagA:r (p.p.)	بغآر	without
baga:run (vi.)	بغارُن	to fry in oil
baga:rI (m.)	بغارٕ	heated edible oil
bagva:n (m.)	بھگوان	God
bagvati: (f.)	بھگوتی	Goddess
baga:vath (m.)	بغاوتھ	revolution
buzun (vt.)	بُزُن	to bake

bacI (m.)	بچہٕ	child/children
bacI nagmI (m.)	بچہٕ نغمہٕ	male dance
bacath (f.)	بچتھ	saving
bacanpa:y (m.)	بچن پاے	way of security
baca:vun (v.m.s.)	بچاوُن	to save, to protect *baca:vIn'* (m.p.,f.s.) *baca:vIni* (f.p.)
bacun (vi.)	بچُن	to escape, to be saved *bacIni* (p)
bajan (m.)	بجن	devotional song
bajar (m.s.)	بجر	greatness, magnanimity
banjar (m.)	بنجر	fallow land
bajA:yi: (f.)	بجآیی	prosperity
baja: (a.)	بجا	prosperous
baja:y (pp.)	بجاے	instead of
baja:vun (m.s.)	بجاوُن	to play (a musical instrument)
bazA:z' (f.)	بزازٕ	cloth
baza:z (m.)	بزاز	cloth merchant
baTI (m.)	بٹہٕ	Kashmiri Pandit
baTIva:r (f.)	بٹہٕ وار	Saturday
baTan' (f.s.)	بٹٕنۍ	Kashmiri pandit woman *baTni* (p)
baTI darIm (m.)	بٹہٕ درم	Hindu religion
baDI (ad)	بڑٕ	very much
baDInA:n' (f.s.)	بڑٕنانۍ	great grandmother
baDIbuD'bab (m.)	بڑٕبُڈۍبب	great grandfather
baDA:yi: (f.)	بڑآیی	greatness, magnanimity
baDun (v.m.s.)	بڑُن	to grow, to proceed *baDIn'* (m.p.,f.s.) *baDIni* (f.p.)
baDa:vun (vt.)	بڑاوُن	to extinguish, to close (shop)
baDra:vun (vt.)	بڑراوُن	to increase, to allow growth
batI (m.)	بتہٕ	cooked rice, food
batIc (f.s.)	بتٕچ	duck *batci* (p)
batI m>Th (m.)	بتہٕ مُوٹھ	handful of cooked rice
batI lej (f.s.)	بتہٕ لیج	pot full of rice
batukh (m.s.)	بطخ	drake *batakh* (p)
bad (a)	بَد	bad
badan (m.)	بدن	body
badIlun (v.m.s.)	بدلُن	to change *badIlIn'* (m.p.,f.s.) *badIlIni* (f.p.)
badIla:vun (v.m.s.)	بدلاوُن	to exchange *badIla:vIn'* (m.p.,f.s.) *badIla:vIni* (f.p.)
badastu:r (ad)	بدستور	continuous, as usual
badkIsmat (a.m.)	بدقسمت	ill lucky
badkIsmati: (f.)	بدقسمتی	misfortune

badtAmi:z (a)	بدتمیز	bad mannered, mischievous
badmiza:z (a)	بدمزاز	bad natured, haughty
badlI (n)	بدلہ	revenge, instead of
badshakII (a)	بدشکل	ugly
badshogu:n (a)	بدشوگون	bad omen
badkhAslath (a)	بدخصلتھ	ill natured, ill mannered
bad calan (a)	بدچلن	immoral, bad charactered
badzan (n)	بدزن	ill intention
badnA:mi: (f.s.)	بدنامی	defame, ignonimy, disrepute
ba~d (m.s.)	بنٛد	dam
banI (m.)	بنہٕ	boundary
bankI (m.)	بنکہٕ	bank
banun (vi.)	بنُن	available, to happen
bana:vun (v.m.s.)	بناوُن	to prepare, to make *bana:vIn'* (m.p.,f.s.) *bana:vIni* (f.p.)
bangikul (m.s.)	بنگہٕ کُل	hemp plant *bangIkul'* (p)
bAngA:l' (a)	بنگاے	Bengali
bangima: (f.)	بنگِما	gesture
banjar (m.)	بنجر	barren, fallow land
band (v)	بنٛد	stanza, close
bandu:kh (m.)	بنٛدوٗق	gun
bandgo:bi: (m.)	بنٛدگوبی	cabbage
bansari: (f.)	بنسری	flute
bab (f.s.)	بَب	breast *babI* (p)
bam (m.)	بٕم	bomb
bar (m.)	بَر	door(s)
barI gatshun (v)	برٕگژھُن	to wither away
baran' (f.s.)	برٕن	main door *barni* (p)
baras tal (n)	برٕس تل	near the door
barun (v.m.s.)	برُن	to fill up, to grieve *barIn'* (m.p.,f.s.) *barIni* (f.p.)
barkh>rda:r (m.)	برخوردار	a young one, loyal
barjast (a)	برجستہ	in full bloom
barphi: (f.)	برفی	a kind of sweet meat
bablva:y (m.)	ببہِ وائے	spasm of breasts
babrikul (m.)	ببرِکُل	basil plant *babrikul'* (p)
bamtsu~:Th (m.)	بمہٕ ژوٗنٛٹھ	quince
bambA:ri (f.)	بم باری	bombardment
bemA:r' (m.)	بیمآری	disease, illness
bema:r (a.m.)	بیمار	patient, sick
bay (m.)	بَے	fear
bakun (vi.)	بکُن	speak angrily, prate
barakas (pp.)	برکس	on the otherhand
bara:dari: (f.)	برادری	brotherhood
bava:si:r (f.)	برادری	piles

bartha: (m.)	بَرتھا	husband
bara:bAri: (f.)	برابری	equality
barda:sh (m.)	بَرداش	tolerance
barsA:t' (f.)	برساتؔ	rain coat
balab (m.)	بلب	lamp
ballvi:r (a.m.)	بلہٕ ویر	brave
balun (v)	بلُن	to recover from illness,
balva:n (a)	بلوان	hero, strong
bale:lI (m.)	بلیلہٕ	belloric myrobalam
bashar (m.)	بشر	human being
basha:shath (f.)	بشاشتھ	joy, happiness
bas (f.s.)	بَس	bus *basI* (p)
basIm (f.)	بٕسم	ashes
basivo:l (f.s.)	بسِہ وول	bus owner *basivA:l'* (p)
basun (v.m.s.)	بسُن	to live, dwell *basIn* (m.p.,f.s.) *basIni* (f.p.)
baski:n (m.)	بسکین	inhabitants, residents
bavun (vi.)	بوُن	be born, grow
baha: (m.)	بہا	steam
baha:r (m.)	بہار	spring (season)
bahas (m.)	بحث	discussion
baha:nI (m.)	بہانہٕ	pretension, excuse
baho:dri: (f.)	بہودری	bravery
banun (vi.)	بنُن	be available, happen
ba:ko:ph (m.)	باکوف	with grandeur, with pomp and show
ba:kama:l (a)	باکمال	excellent, with excelence
ba:kh (f.s.)	باکھ	• funeral weeping, crying *ba:kI* (p)
ba:g (m.)	باغ	garden
ba:gIva:n (m.)	باغٕوان	gardner
ba:giva:n (m.)	باگہِ وان	lucky (person)
ba~:g (f.)	بانگ	the voice of the Muazin (call for prayer by Muslims)
ba:jI (m.)	باجہٕ	musical instrument
ba:jama:th (ad)	باجماتھ	together, in congregation
ba:z (m.)	باز	falcon
ba:zA:bti (ad.)	بازآبتہٕ	regularly
ba:ze: (ad)	باضے	sometimes
ba:zar (m.)	بازر	market
ba~:D (m.)	بانڈ	folk dance performers
ba~:DIjAshIn (m.)	بانڈٕجشن	folk song and drama entermainment
ba~:dav (m.)	باندو	relative
ba:nIvo:l (m.)	بانہٕ وول	shopkeeper who sells the utensils

ba:da:m (m.)	بادام	almond(s)
ba:da:mkul (m.s.)	بادام کُل	almond tree *ba:da:mkul'* (p)
bada:m po:sh (m.)	بادام پوش	almond flower
ba:nI (m.)	بانہٕ	utensil(s)
ba:nIkuTh (m.s.)	بانہٕ کُٹھ	store room *ba:nIkuTh'* (p)
ba:path (p.p.)	باپتھ	for
ba:pA:r' (m.)	باپأری	businessman
ba:pa:r (m.)	باپار	business
ba:pasha:kh (a)	باپوشاکھ	in full dress
ba~:bIr (ad)	بامبٕر	hurry, haste
ba:pAthIr (m.)	باپتھٕر	brother's son, nephew
ba:m (m.s.)	بام	a kind of roof (filled with earth)
ba:ma:ne: (a)	بامانے	meaningful
ba:r (m.)	بار	responsibility, burden
ba:r (m.)	بار	bar
ba:rIn' (m.)	بارٕنؠ	brothers, brethern
ba:rat (m.)	بارت	India
ba:rav (m.)	بارو	wild cry
ba:rda:nI (m.)	باردانہٕ	package, gunny bags
ba:l (m.)	بال	mountain
ba:l (f.)	بال	ball
ba:lIthong (m.s.)	بالہٕ ٹھونگ	mountain top, peak of the mountain
ba:lIda:man (m.)	بالہٕ دامن	bottom of the hill/ mountain
ba:lIpa:n (m.)	بالہٕ پان	childhood, youthful bloom
ba:leg (m.)	بالیغ	matured, major
ba:lTi:n (m.)	بالٹین	bucket
ba:v (m.)	باو	cost
ba:vun (v.m.s.)	باوُن	to offer,to divulge *ba:vIn'* (m.p.,f.s.) *ba:vIni* (f.p.)
ba:vna: (f.)	باونا	feeling
ba:vaju:d (p.p.)	باوجود	inspite of
ba:vrI (a.m.)	باوٕر	mad
ba:sha:n (a)	باشان	with grandeur
ba:shi (m.p.)	باشہِ	the language of infants
ba:shI karni (vi.)	باشہٕ کرنہِ	to speak (speech of a baby)
ba:sun (v.m.s.)	باسُن	to feel *ba:sIn'* (m.p.,f.s.) *ba:sIni* (f.p.)
ba:sIna:vun (v.m.s.)	باسہٕ ناوُن	to make (someone) feel *ba:sIna:vIn'* (m.p.,f.s.) *ba:sIna:vIni* (f.p.)
ba:s d'un (v)	باس دِیُن	to make one feel
ba:smath (f.)	باسمتھ	a variety of rice
ba:h (a)	باہ	twelve

bikhA:r' (f.s.)	بِکھآرِ	beggar
bicur (m.)	بِچُر	hairlock, forelock *bicIr'* (p)
bico:r (a)	بِچور	poor, simple fellow
biTh (f.)	بِٹھ	crowd
bilI (a.)	بِلہٕ	green eyed person
bilkul (ad)	بِلکُل	at all, quite
bila:ija:zat	بلا اجازت	without permission
bil'bicur (m.)	بلی بچُر	bulbul, nightingale
bistarI (m.)	بِسترٕ	bedding/beddings
bistarI band (m.)	بستر بنٛد	bedcover, holdall
bihun (v.m.)	بِہُن	to sit
biga:run (vi.)	بِگارُن	to spoil
bi:n (f.)	بیٖن	veena, bag pipe
bi:r (f.)	بیٖر	crowd, beer
bi:rI (m.)	بیٖرٕ	small wooden ball
begA:r' (f.)	بیگآرِ	bonded labour
bedi:n (a.)	بے دین	athiest
beni (f.)	بێنہِ	sister/sisters
be~zI (f.)	بێنٛزٕ	sister's daughter
benthIr (m.)	بێنٛتھٕر	sister's son
beDo:l (a)	بے ڈول	ugly, asymmetrical
beme:l (a)	بے میل	not matching
beyi (ad)	بێیہِ	also, moreover, again
beyilaTi (ad)	بێیہِ لٹہِ	sometime again, at another time
beyi vAriyi (ad)	بێیہِ ؤرِیہِ	next year
beyi sa:tI (ad)	بێیہِ ساتہٕ	next time
behtAri: (f.)	بہتری	betterment
behna:vun (v.m.s.)	بہناوُن	to make sit, to convince *behna:vIn'* (m.p.,f.s.) *behna:vIni* (f.p.)
behva:r (f.)	بیہوار	open place for village cattle
behva:l (m.)	بیہوال	idle person, shirker
be:avla:d (a.)	بے اولاد	childless
be:kIl (a)	بیقل	fool
be:kas (a)	بیکس	supportless, destitute
be:ka:r	بیکار	useless, unemployed
be:kara:r (m.)	بے قرار	restless
be:guna:h (a)	بے گناہ	innocent
be:chI (n)	بیچھہٕ	beggar
be:chun (v.m.s.)	بیچھُن	to beg *be:chIn'* (m.p.,f.s.) *be:chIni* (f.p.)
be:zti: (f.)	بے عزتی	insult, humiliation
be:za:r (n)	بیزار	angry, disgusted
be:tA:bi: (f.)	بے تآبی	impatience
be:ta:b (a)	بے تاب	impatient
be:to:r (a)	بے تور	odd, ill mannered (person)
be:dA:ri: (f.)	بے دآری	awakening
be:pana:h (a)	بے پناہ	unlimited, limitless
be:phikir (a)	بے فکِر	careless, without worry

be:phrok (a)	بےپھرٕک	without worry, free from worry
be:mI (m.)	بیمہٕ	sister's husband
be:r (f.s.)	بیر	demarcation line (of a field) parapet *be:rI* (p)
be:ra:m (a)	بیمار	sick
be:l (m.)	بیل	shovel, spade
be:lan (m.)	بیلن	chapati roller
be:vaphA:yi: (a)	بےوفائی	faithlessness, disloyality treachery
be:va:yi (a)	بےوایہ	without hindrance
be:shak (ad)	بےشک	doubtless
be:shu:b (a)	بےشۆب	ugly, ill mannered
be:sharIm (a)	بےشرم	shameless
be:su:d (ad)	بےسوٗد	in vain
be:sabri: (f.)	بےصبری	impatience
beho:sh (a)	بےہوش	unconscious
b'uch (m.)	بیٚچھ بِچھ	scorpion *bich'* (p)
buchun (vt.)	بُچھُن	to sting
bujar (m.)	بُجر	old age
busun (vi.)	بُسُن	be pale
buzun (v.m.s.)	بُزُن	to roast (grain, mutton, etc) *buzIn'* (m.p.,f.s.) *buzIni* (f.p.)
buzIna:vun (v.m.s.)	بُزناوُن	to get roasted *buzIna:vIn'* (m.p.,f.s.) *buzIna:vIni* (f.p.)
buzdil (a)	بُزدِل	coward
buD (f.s.)	بُڈ	old woman *buji* (p)
buDI (m.s.p.)	بُڈ	old man/old men
buDun (v.m.s.)	بُڈُن	to become old *buDIn'* (m.p.,f.s.) *buDIni* (f.p.)
buD'bab (m.)	بُڈٕبب	grandfather
but (m.)	بُت	image, idol
butra:th (f.)	بُتراتھ	earth
butshikan (n)	بُت شِکن	iconoclast, idol breaker
buth (m.s.)	بُتھ	face *buth'* (p)
buthi (ad)	بُتھِ	in front of
buth phirun (v)	بُتھ پھِرُن	to refuse, to disobey, to scold, chide
budul (m.)	بُدُل	silver fir
bun'ul (m.)	بُنیُل	earthquake
bunil'yaTh (m.s.)	بُنِلی یٹھ	tremor
buniya:d (f.)	بُنیاد	foundation, base
bumsim (n)	بُم سِم	earthworm
bum (f.s.)	بُم	eyebrow *bumI* (p)
burI (a)	بُر	bad
burush (m.)	بُرُش	brush
burzIkul (m.s.)	بُرزِکُل	birch tree *burzIkul'* (p)

burbatan (f.s.)	بُربٹن	top-toy *burbatIni* (p)
buhIr' (f.)	بُہرِ	jute bag, gunny bag*bohri* (p)
buhur (m.)	بُہُر	a grocer, performer
bu:gun (vi)	بوٗگُن	to enjoy
bu:Th (m.)	بوٗٹھ	shoe(s)
bu:t (m.)	بوٗت	ghost, devil
bu:n' (f.)	بوٗنۍ	a maple tree *bo:ni* (p)
boch (a.m.s.)	بۄچھ	hungry *boch'* (p)
b>chi hot (a.m.s.)	بۆچھ ہۆت	hungry *b>ochi hAt'* (p)
boTh (m.s.)	بۄٹھ	bank of a river *bATh'* (p)
boD (a.m.s.)	بۄڈ	big *bAD'* (p) *bAD* (f.s.) *baji* (p)
boD doh (m.)	بۄڈ دوہ	festival
boD bADi:m (ad)	بۄڈ بڈیم	at the most
boD ba:rI (a)	بۄڈ بارِ	very heavy, very big
b>nI (ad)	بوٚنہٕ	below
b>Dun (vi.)	بوٚڈُن	to sink
bonIga:m (m.)	بوٚنہٕ گام	the lower part of the village
bombur (m.s.)	بومبُر	black bee *bombar* (p)
bomva:r (f.)	بوموار	Tuesday

bos (m.s.)	بۄس	husk
bohgun (m.)	بۄہگُن	a pot *bohgan* (p)
bohrun (v.m.s.)	بۄہرُن	to dare *bohrIn'* (m.p.,f.s.) *bohrIni* (f.p.)
bo:j (m.)	بوج	weight
bo:zInI yun (v)	بوزنہٕ یُن	to see, to be seen
bo:zun (v.m.s.)	بوزُن	to hear *bo:zIn'* (m.p.,f.s.) *bo:zIni* (f.p.)
bo:zanvA:l' (m.)	بوزن وأل	audience
ba:zIna:vun (v.m.s.)	بوزناوُن	to make (someone) hear *bo:zIna:vIn'* (m.p.,f.s.) *bo:zIna:vIni* (f.p.)
bo:tal (f.)	بوتل	bottle/bottles
b'on b'on (ad)	بیۄن بیۄن	separately
bo:y (m.s.)	بوے	brother *bA:y* (p)
bo:r (m.s.)	بور	luggage, burden
bo:lun (v.m.s.)	بولُن	to speak *bo:lIn'* (m.p.,f.s.) *bo:lIni* (f.p.)
bo:sh (m.)	بوش	pride
b>d (f.)	بوٚد	wisdom
bkvAT (f.s.)	بوٚک وٹ	kidney *bkvaci* (p)
b>n (ad)	بوٚن	down

b>dva:r (f.)	بۄدوار	Wednesday
b>vun (v.m.s.)	بۄوُن	to grow *b>vIn'* (m.p.,f.s.) *b>vIni* (f.p.)
brimjikul (m.s.)	برِمجِکُل	celtis australis tree *brimjikul'* (p)
bram (m.)	برم	doubt, to mistake something for another thing
bramun (vi.)	برمُن	be tempted, covet
bramIrun (vi.)	برمہٕ رُن	be misled
bramIra:vun (vi.)	برمہٕ راوُن	to mislead
brakun (vt.)	برکُن	masticate, crunch with teeth, be angry
brA~:D' (f.)	برانڈِ	brandy
brA~:D' (f.s.)	برانڈِ	over coat *bra~:Di* (p)
bra:~dI kAn' (f.s.)	برانٛدِ کٔنۍ	stone of verandah
baha:l karun (v.m.)	بحال کرُن	to reinstate
bri~ja:bI (m.)	برنٛجابہٕ	rice water
breyi po:sh (n)	بریہِ پوش	jujube flower
brA:r (f.s.)	براٗر	she cat *bra:ri* (p)
brA:Thun (v.m.s.)	براٗٹھن	to become stupid, to lose wisdom *brA:ThIn'* (m.p.,f.s.) *brA:ThIni* (f.p.)
brag (m.)	برگ	heron
branIkul (m.s.)	برنہٕ کُل	elm *branIkul'* (p)
bramIra:vun (v.m.s.)	برمہٕ راوُن	to deceive *bramIra:vIn'* (m.p.,f.s.) *bramIra:vIni* (f.p.)
brasva:r (f.)	برسوار	Thursday
bra~:d (m.)	برانٛڑ	verandah, entrance floor of a house
breyi (f.p.)	بریہِ	berry
brisla:y	برِس لاے	fishing rod
bru~z (m.)	برُنٛز	moment
bro:r (m.)	بروٗر	he cat *brA:r'* (p)
bru~:him (a)	برُونٛہِم	of earlier times, old
bro~:Th (ad)	برونٛٹھ	before, infront
bro~:Th kun (ad)	برونٛٹھ کُن	forward, in future

m

mItsIra:vun (v.m.s.)	مِژراوُن	to open *mItsIra:vIn'* (m.p.,f.s.) *mItsIra:vIni* (f.p.)
mItsrun (vt.)	مِژرُن	to open
mIthIr (m.)	مِتھِر	urine
mIslI (m.)	مِسلہٕ	hide, skin
mAtsIra:vun (v.m.s.)	مٔژراوُن	to make someone mad *mAtsIra:vIn'* (m.p.,f.s.) *mAtsIra:vIni* (f.p.)

mAch (f.s.)	مٕچھ	fly *machi* (p)
mAjlis (f.s.)	مٕجلس	committee, meeting, gathering *mAjlisI* (p)
mAjlu:n (m.)	مٕجلوٗن	Majnun -a legendry lover
mazi:d (a)	مزید	more
ma~zil (m.)	مٔنزِل	destination
mAT (f.s.)	مٕٹ	big vessel *maci* (p)
mAdIr (a)	مٕدٕر	sweat
mAdre:r (m.s.)	مٕدریر	sugar
mAnDi: (f.)	مٕنڈی	market
mAnisTar (m.)	مٕنِسٹر	minister
mAr'da:dum (a)	مٕرِدیادم	elderly man
mAshrun (v.m.s.)	مٕشرُن	cause to forget *mAshrIn'* (m.p.,f.s.) *mAshrIni* (f.p.)
mAshi:d (f.)	مٕشید	mosque *mAshi:dI* (p)
mAshi:r (m.)	مٕشیر	adviser
mAshra:vun (v.m.s.)	مٕشراوُن	to forget *mAshra:vIn'* (m.p.,f.s.) *mAshra:vIni* (f.p.)
mAhlI (m.)	مٕحلہٕ	mohalla
mAhalda:r (m.)	مٕحل دار	assesser, a guard (in excise deptt.)
mAhla:mI (m.)	مٕحلامہٕ	ointment
mA:j (s.)	ماج	mother *ma:ji* (p)
mA:zi: (ad)	ماضی	past time
mA~:ziDul (m.)	ماٗنزِڈُل	mrytle pot
mA~:zim yo:r (m.)	ماٗنزِم یور	middleman
mA~:zira:th (f.)	ماٗنزِراتھ	mrytle ceremony (during night)
mA:dI (m.s.)	ماٗدٕ	fine flour
mA:da:n (m.)	ماٗدان	plain, field
mA:r (f.)	ماٗر	tributary
mA:r'mo~d (a)	ماٗری موند	beautiful
mA:l (m.)	ماٗل	appetite
mA:lI (a)	ماٗلہٕ	dirty
mA:lI (m.)	ماٗلہٕ	fair
mA:lIgi: (f.)	ماٗلہٕ گی	dirtyness
mA:likh (m.)	ماٗلکھ	owner/owners
mA:lish (f.s.)	ماٗلش	massage
mA:lyi (f.)	ماٗلیہ	land revenue
mA:sh (f.s.)	ماٗش	she buffaloe *mA:shi* (p)
mA:shikrA:r (f.s)	ماٗشِہ کرٲر	a milk product *mA:shikra:ri* (p)
mA:shikoT (m.s.)	ماٗشِہ کوٹ	he buffaloe *mA:shikAT'* (p)
mA:sho:k (a)	ماٗشوق	beloved
mA:hir (a)	ماٗہِر	expert

makIts (f.s.)	مۄکٕژ	axe *makItsI* (p)
maka:n (m.s.)	مکان	a house
makA:y (m.)	مکآے	maize corn
maka:yi kul (m.s.)	مکایہٕ کُل	maize plant *maka:ya kul'* (p)
maka:yivAT (f.s.)	مکائیہ وُٹ	corn-cob
maktab (m.)	مکتَب	a basic school
makbu:l (a)	مقبوٗل	famous, popular
maksad (m.)	مقصَد	purpose
magI (n)	مۄگہٕ	whiskers
ma~gtI (a)	منٛگتہٕ	adapted
ma~gtI necuv (m.)	منٛگتہٕ نیچُو	adopted son/ daughter *ma~gtI neciv* (p)
magpharath (m.)	مغفرَت	salvation
magarmatsh (m.)	مگرمژھ	crocodile
ma~ gun (v)	منٛگُن	to ask. to beg
magrib (m.)	مغرِب	west
magribi: (a)	مغربی	western
machardA:n' (f.s.)	مچھر دآنۍ	mosquito net *macharda:ni* (p)
matsar (a)	مَژر	madness
matsh (f.)	مَژھ	mince meat
maja:l (a)	مجال	possible, ability, power
manz (pp.)	منٛز	inside
mazI (m.)	مزٕ	taste
mazIhar (m.)	مزہر	plague
maza:kh (m.)	مزاق	joke
maza:r (m.s.)	مزار	graveyards
maza:rI po:sh (m.)	مزارہٕ پوش	the flowers that grow on the graveyard
mazbu:th (a)	مضبوٗط	strong
mazmath (f.)	مزمت	criticism
mazmu:n (m.)	مضموٗن	essay
mazhab (m.)	مذہب	religion
maTar (m.)	مٹر	peas
mashun (v)	مشُن	to forget
matun (vi.)	متُن	be mad
mathun (v.m.s.)	متھُن	to rub *mathIn'* (m.p.,f.s.) *mathIni* (f.p.)
mad (a)	مَد	pride
madadga:r (a.)	مدد گار	helper
madIrA:s' (a.)	مدرآسی	Madrasi
mandiyan (ad)	مندیَن	afternoon, noontide
madho:sh (a)	مدہوش	intoxicated
mamnun (vi.)	ممنُن	to become senseless (of a limb)
man (m.)	مَن	mond - about 40 Kgs., mind
manA:r' (f.)	منآری	grocery

mana:vun (v.m.s.)	مناوُن	to celebrate *mana:vIn'* (m.p.,f.s.) *mana:vIni* (f.p.)
mangun (v.m.s.)	منٛگُن	to ask for something, demand, beg *mangIn'* (m.p.,f.s.) *mangIni* (f.p.)
mane:jar (m.)	منیجر	manager
manz-athI (m.)	منٛزٕ اتھہٕ	palm/palms
manzI manzI (ad)	منٛزٕ منٛزٕ	sometimes
manzul (m.)	منٛزل	cradle *manzIl'* (p)
mandIchun (v.m.s.)	منٛدٕچھُن	to be shy, feel ashamed *mandIchin'* (m.p.,f.s.) *mandIchini* (f.p.)
mandul/mandal (m.)	مُنٛڈُل/منڈل	buttocks
mandar (m.)	منٛدر	temple/temples
mandun (vi.)	مُنٛدُن	to churn (milk)
mandchun (vi.)	منٛدٕچھُن	be ashamed
mansu:bI (m.)	منصوٗبہٕ	plan
manhu:s (a)	منحوٗس	abominable
mable:l (m.)	مبلیل	mobil-oil
manmA:ni: (f.)	من مآنی	of one's own choice, willfulness
may (m.)	مےٚ	liquor
maya:r (a)	معیار	standard

magmu:n (m.)	مغموٗن	sad
marIg (m.)	مٔرٕگ	death
martsIphol (m.s.)	مرٕژپھول	a corn of black pepper *martsIphAl'* (p)
martsIva~:gun (m.)	مرٕژوانٛگن	chilly
marIz (m.)	مٔرٕض	disease
marId (m.)	مٔرٕد	male, man
marnIsar (a)	مرنہٕ سر	on death bed
marIhu:m (a)	مرحوٗم	dead person
marzi: (m.)	مرضی	wish, desire
marag (m.)	مٔرگ	pasture, meadow
martIba:nI (m.)	مرتبانہٕ	jar
marun (v.m.s.)	مرُن	to die *marIn'* (m.p.,f.s.) *marIni* (f.p.)
marham (m.)	مرہم	ointment
mara:z (m.)	مراز	north-eastern part of the valley
mal (m.)	مل	dirt
mallI (m.)	ملہٕ	a Muslim priest
mallIr (f.s.)	ملٕر	pitcher *mallri* (p)
malA:y (f.)	ملآے	cream
malakh (m.)	ملکھ	angles
mala:lI (m.)	ملالہٕ	defection, insult, grief
malun (v.m.s.)	ملُن	to rub

malmal (f.) مَلمَل muslin

maval (m.) مَوَل mane

mashA:l' (f.s.) مشاگ torch, two or more gas lamps fixed in one handle, lights *masha:li* (p)

mashi:ni: (a) مشینی mechanical

mashrikh (m.) مشرِق east

mashIk (f.s.) مَشق wooden slate *mashkI* (p)

mashun (vi.) مشُن to forget

mas (m.) مَس hair

masIkhar (a) مَسخر commedian

masa:lI (m.) مَصالہ spices

mahakam (a) محکم strong

mahaz (ad) مجاز only

maha: (f.) مہا black gram, vetch

maha:z (m.) مہاز front

mahdu:d (a) مہدوُد limited

mahphu:m (m.) مہفوُم connotation, subject-matter, core idea

ma:hra:zI (m.) مہراز bridegroom

ma:hren' (f.) ماہرینی bride

ma:g (m.) ماگ Magh, name of a tenth month of Bikrami era

ma~:gay (f.) مانگے a kind of demand

ma:ch (m.) ماچھ honey

ma:chtullr (m.) ماچھ تُلر honey bee

ma~:jun (v.m.s.) مانجُن to cleanse utencils *ma~:jin'* (m.p.,f.s.) *ma~:jini* (f.p.)

ma:zun (vt.) مازُن make clean, sweep over

ma:z (m.) ماز flesh, mutton, meat

ma:zan (m.) مازن rough broom

ma:zbe:r (f.s.) مازبیر gam *ma:zbe:rI* (p)

ma:Th (m.) ماٹھ destination

ma:tam (m.) ماتم mourning

mata:ma:l (m.) ماتامال mother's parental house

m'a:dI (m.) معدہ/میادہ stomach

ma:dI (a.) مادہ female

ma:dIparas (a) مادہ پرس materialist

ma:n (m.) مان respect

ma:nun (vi.) مانُن to admit

ma:nun (v.m.s.) مانُن to accept, to agree *ma:nIn'* (m.p.,f.s.) *ma:nIni* (f.p.)

ma:~nDun (vt.m.s.) مانڈُن to knead (flour) mix *ma:nDIn'* (m.p.,f.s.) *ma:nDIni* (f.p.)

ma:p (m.) ماپ measurement

ma:ph (m.) معاف pardon, excuse

ma:m (m.) مام maternal uncle

ma:man' ( ) مامنی maternal aunt *ma:mIni* (p)

ma:mlI (m.) معاملہ matter

ma:y (f.)	ماے	love
ma:yi (m.)	مایہ	paste
ma:ya:na:z (a)	مایاناز	cause of pride, of higher standard
ma:yir (f.)	مایِر	a kind of saltish curds and rice preparation
ma:yu:si: (f.)	مایوٗسی	disappointment
ma:rIna:vun (v.m.s.)	مارٕناوُن	to get someone killed *m:rIna:vIn'* (m.p.,f.s.) *ma:rIna:vIni* (f.p.)
ma:rIva:tul (m.s.)	مارٕواتُل	executioner, hangman
ma:run (v.m.s.)	مارُن	to kill *ma:rIn'* (m.p.,f.s.) *ma:rIni* (f.p.)
ma:rIc (m.)	مارٕچ	March
ma:l (m.)	مال	goods, cargo, materials, property
ma:l (f.)	مال	garland, rosary
ma:l'un (m.)	مالۍُن	parental house for married woman
ma:lda:r (m.)	مالدار	prosperous, rich
ma:vas (f.)	ماوَس	amavasya
ma:s (f.s.)	ماس	mother's sister *ma:sI* (p)
ma:suv (m.s.)	ماسُو	mother's sister's husband *ma:sIv'* (p)
ma:sTar (m.)	ماسٹر	teacher
ma:sTarba:y (f.s.)	ماسٹربائے	lady teacher, teacher's wife *ma:sTar ba:yi* (p)
ma:stIrbeni (f.)	ماسترٕبینہٕ	mother's sister's daughter
ma:stur bo:y (m.s.)	ماسُتربوے	mother's sister's son *ma:stIr' bA:y* (p)
miza:j (m.)	مِزاج	health, welfare, temparament, mood
miTun (v)	مِٹُن	to erased, be finished
miThA:y (f.)	مِٹھاے	sweets
minaTh (m.)	مِنٹھ	minute
minath (f.)	مِنَتھ	obligation
miyi (m.)	مِیہِ	Kshetri, Kashmiri Rajput *miyi ba:y* (f.s.) *miyi ba:yi* (p)
mil (f.s.)	مِل	mill
millr (f.s.)	مِلِر	a roll
millna:vun (vt.m.s.)	مِلہٕ ناوُن	to mix, to join *millna:vIn'* (m.p.,f.s.) *millna:vIni* (f.p.)
millvA:r (f.s.)	مِلہٕ وآر	a pot for grey clay *millva:ri* (p)
mila:vaTh (f.s.)	مِلاوَٹھ	adulteration
milkiyath (f.)	مِلکیتھ	ancestral property
miltsa:r (m.)	مِلہٕ ژار	integration, harmony
mishi:n gan (m.)	مشین گن	machine gun
mishi:nivo:l (m.s.)	مشینہٕ وول	one who owns a machine *mishi:nivA:l'* (p)

misal (f.s.)	مِسل	file *misll* (p)
miski:n (a)	مِسکین	poor
miski:ni: (m.)	مِسکینی	poverty
miskhora:sa:n (m.)	مِسکھوراسان	aluminium
mistAr' (m.)	میستٕری	technician
misrI (m.)	مِصرٕ	a line of the song
misva:kh (m.)	مِسواکھ	stick for cleaning teeth, tooth brush
mi:za:n (m.)	میزان	total
mi:m (f.s.)	میم	an English woman *mi:mI* (p)
mi:l (f.)	میل	ink
mi:l (m.)	میل	mile
mi:lIpAT (f.s.)	میلہٕ پٔٹ	milestone
mi:lIva:dan (ad)	میلہٕ وادن	miles together
mi:li dava:t (f.s.)	میلہٕ دوات	inkpot *mi:li davA:ts* (p)
m'ekna:ti:z (m.)	میکناتیز	magnet
mekda:r (m.)	میقدار	quantity
me:kh (f.s.)	میکھ	nail, peg
me~gun (m.s.)	میگُن	sheep dung, dropping *me~gan* (p)
mA:c (m.)	ماچ	match
mets (f.)	میژ	clay, earth
metsiti:l (m.)	میژہ تیل	kerosene oil
meT (f.)	مٔٹ	handful of food
mevI (m.)	میوٕ	dry fruit, fruit
mehnat kash (a)	محنت کش	hard worker
mehra:jul a:lam (m.)	معراج العالم	a Muslim festival
me:khal (f.)	میکھل	sacred thread ceremony of Hindus
me:z (m.)	میز	table
me:zpo:sh (m.)	میز پوش	table cloth
me:zba:n (m.)	میزبان	host
me:Th (m.)	میٹھ	a person who is incharge of labourers, contractor
me:Thun (vi.)	میٹھُن	be sweet
me:nun (v.m.s.)	مینُن	to measure *me:nIn'* (m.p.,f.s.) *me:nIni* (f.p.)
me: (m.)	مئے	May
me:lun (v.m.s.)	میلُن	to get, to meet *me:lIn'* (m.p.,f.s.) *me:lIni* (f.p.)
mehma:n navA:zi: (f.)	مہمان نوازی	entertainment for guests
me:hma:r (m.)	میمار	builder, mason
mukadar (m.)	مقدر	luck
mukarar (a)	مقرر	fixed, definite, posted
muka:balI (m.)	مقابلہٕ	competition, face
mukhA:liphath (m.)	مخالفت	opposition

mutsIrun (v.m.s.)	مُژرُن	to open *mutsIrIn'* (m.p.,f.s.) *mutsI,Ini* (f.p.)
mutsakari: (f.)	مُژھکری	mutual dispute, antagonism
muj (f.s.)	مُج	raddish *muji* (p)
mujA:hid (m.)	مجاہد	war warrior, crusador
mujrim (m.)	مُجرم	culprit
muzir (a)	مُضر	bad
muTh (m.)	مُٹھ	soyabean
muDI (a)	مُڈ	illiterate
mutIvA:tir (ad)	مُتواتر	continuously
mutA:bik (pp.)	مُطابق	according to
mutA:sir (a)	متاثر	influenced
mutmAyi:n (a)	مطمئن	satisfied
mutalakh (pp.)	مُتلق	about
muthadi maha:z (m.)	مُتحدی محاذ	united front
muta:lI (m.)	مُطالہ	study
mudav (m.)	مُدو	back soar of horses
munazam (a)	منظم	organised
munispalTi: (f.)	مُنسپلٹی	municipality
muma:pha: (m.)	مُنافع	profit
muma:phIkho:r (m.)	مُنافع خور	profiteer
munA:sib (a)	مناسب	proper
munsiph (m.)	منصف	munsif, - judge
munun (v.m.s.)	مُنُن	to husk, to beat *munIn'* (m.p.,f.s.) *munIni* (f.p.)
muphi:d (a)	مُفید	useful
muba:rakh (m.)	مُبارکھ	congratulations
mumkin (a)	مُمکن	possible
mura:d (m.)	مُراد	desire, objective
mulIkh (m.)	مُلکھ	country
mulA:zim (m.)	مُلازم	employee
mula:ka:th (m.)	مُلاقات	meeting
multAvi: (f.)	مُلتوی	postponement
mush (m.)	مُش	fist
mushkil (m.)	مُشکل	difficulty *mushkila:t* (p)
mushtarkI (a)	مشترکہ	common
musha:yri (m.)	مُشاعرہ	poetical symposium
musur (m.)	مُسُر	lentils
mustakIbIl (a)	مستقبل	future
muhim (m.)	مُہم	expedition, problem, project
muhur (m.)	مُہُر	a poisonous insect (cater piller) *muhIr'* (p)
muhul (m.s.)	مُہُول	pounding pestke *muhIl'* (p)
muhu:rath (m.)	مہورت	auspicious time

muhril (m.)	مُہرِل	clerk, despatcher
mu:c (m.)	موٗچ	cobbler
mu:ju:d (a)	موٗجوٗد	existent, exist, available
m'u:Th (a.m.s.)	میوٗٹھ	sweet *mi:Th'* (m.p.) *mi:Th* (f.s.) *me:chi* (f.p.)
mu:r (f.s.)	موٗر	a thin stick *mu:rI* (p)
mu:rukh (a.m.s.)	موٗرکھ	fool *mu:rakh* (p.)
mu:l (m.)	موٗل	root
mu:li: (ad)	موٗلی	originally
mu:si:ki: (f.)	موٗسیقی	music
mokur (m.)	موٚکُر	dirty, corpse of an animal
mokja:r (m.)	موکجار	leisure, divorce
m>kh (m.)	موکھ	face
m>khti:	موکھتی	deliverance
mcar (m.)	موچہر	thickness, obesity
m>tsun (v.m.s.)	موژُن	to shrink, remain *m>tsIn'* (m.p.,f.s.) *m>tsIni* (f.p.)
mozu:r' (m.)	موزوٗری	labour charges
mozu:r (m.)	موزوٗر	labourer
moT (a.m.s.)	موٚٹ	fat, thick *moT'* (p) *moT* (f.s.) *m>ci* (f.p.)
modur (a.m.s.)	موٚدُر	sweet *mAdIr'* (m.p.) *mAdIr* (f.s.) *mAdIri* (f.p.)
monD (m.)	موٚنڈ	log of wood
mot (a.m.s.)	موٚت	mad man *mAt'* (p) *mAts* (f.s.) *matsI* (f.p.)
m>mI (m.)	موٚمہ	breast(s)
momIr (f.s.)	موٚمہر	penis (of grown up men)
m>y (m.)	موے	wine
m>yIva:l (m.)	موہِوال	single hair
mor (m.)	موٚر	cage, hencoop
m>rbI (m.)	موربہ	jam
moh (m.s.)	موہ	mosquito *mAh'* (p)
mohta:j (a)	موٚحتاج	needy, destitute
moh ma:ya: (f.)	موہ مایا	attraction of worldly things
mohram (m.)	موٚحرم	Muslim Shiya festival, first month of Hijri era
mo:ku:l (a)	موقوٗل	proper
mo:zI (m.)	موزٕ	socks
mo:zu:n (a)	موزوٗن	appropriate, suitable
mo:Tar (m.)	موٹر	motor, car
mo:D (m.)	موڑ	bend
mo:tal (m.)	موتل	suspend
mo:tabar (a)	موتبر	confidante, elderly, wise
m'o:n (pr.m.s.)	میوون	mine, my *me:n'* (m.p.,f.s.) *m'a:ni* (f.p.)

mo:mbAt' (f.s.)	موم بتۍ	wax candle *mo:mbati* (p)
mo:mu:li: (a)	معموٗلی	ordinary
mo:r (m.)	موٗر	peacock
mo:rpakh (m.)	موٗرپکھ	feather of peacock
mo:ru:ph (a)	موٗرٗوف	well-known
mo:l (m.s.)	موٗل	father *mA:l'* (p)
mo:lvi: (m.)	موٗلوی	priest (Muslim)
mo:sam (m.)	موٗسم	weather, season
mo:su:m (a)	موٗسوٗم	innocent
m>kIlun (v.m.s.)	موٗکلُن	to be free, to be over, to be finished *mkIlIn'* (m.p.,f.s.) *mkIlIni* (f.p.)
m>kIla:vun (v.m.s.)	موٗکلاوُن	to finish *mkIla:vIn'* (m.p.,f.s.) *mkIla:vIni* (f.p.)
m>kul (a.m.s.)	موٗکُل	free *mkIl'* (m.p.) *mkIj* (f.s.) *mkIji* (f.p.)
m>kh (m.)	موٗکھ	mouth, face
m>khI (pp.)	موٗکھہِ	for
m>khtI (m.)	موٗختہٕ	pearl
m>khta:r (a)	موٗختار	all in all
m>khsar (ad)	موٗخصر	in short
m>Tun (vi.)	موٗٹُن	become fat
m>Tun (vi.)	موٗٹُن	to agree
m~g (m.)	موٗنگ	moong
m>tsun (v.m.s.)	موٗژُن	to remain, to be left, reduced to *mtsIn'* (m.p.,f.s.) *mtsIni* (f.p.)
m>nD (f.)	موٗنڈ	widow
m>nDun (vi.)	موٗنڈُن	be blunt, weak
m>njiho:r (m.)	موٗنجہ ہور	Maghar, name of the eighth month of Bikrami era
m>rdI (m.)	موٗردٕ	dead body
m>l (m.)	موٗل	value
mIlj (a.f.)	موٗلج	costly
m>va:d (m.s.)	موٗاد	subject matter

y

yAtskA:l' (ad)	یٔژکالۍ	after a long time
yAzman (m.)	یٔزمن	host, bride's/bridegroom's father
yAzman ba:y (f.)	یٔزمن بایے	bride's/bridegroom's mother
yAT (f.s.)	یٔٹ	a basket used for carrying load on shoulders *yeci* (p)
yADal (a)	یٔڈل	glutton
yAD do:d (m.s.)	یٔڈدود	stomach ache
yenivo:l (m.)	ییٚنہٕ وول	bridegroom's party
yAndIr (m.)	یٔندر	spinning wheel

yAndrItul (m.s.)	ینٛدرٕژتُل	spool of spinning wheel
yA:r (f.s.)	یآر	pine tree *ya:ri* (p)
yA:ri: (f.)	یآری	kindness, blessing
yakI (f.p.)	یکہٕ	vomitting
yaki:n (m.)	یقیٖن	belief, confidence
yakba:r (ad)	یکبار	at a time
yakh (a)	یخ	cold
yakhIn' (f.)	یخنۍ	a meat dish cooked in curds
yakh ta:r (m.)	یکتار	single stringed musical istrument
yakhla:k (m.)	یخلاق	character
yakh mush (ad)	یکہ مش	at once, at a stretch
yag' (m.)	یگۍ	yajna
yagIja: (ad)	یگجا	together
yatshun (v.m.s.)	یژھُن	to desire, to wish *yatshIn'* (m.p.,f.s.) *yatshIni* (f.p.)
yazath (m.)	یزتھ	prestige, respect
yaza:z (m.)	یزاز	degree, honour
yach (m.)	یچھ	yaksha
yaTh (f.)	یٹھ	jerk
yaD (f.)	یڈ	belly
yat'ath (ad)	یتیتھ	here (locational)
yath damas ta:m (ad)	یتھ دمس تام	upto this moment
yath baja:yi (ad)	یتھ بجایہ	instead of this
yana:m (m.)	ینام	prize
yangI (m.)	ینگہٕ	asafoetida
yantIr (m.)	ینترٕ	machine, amulet
yapA:r' (ad)	یپآرۍ	in this direction
yamra:zI (m.)	یمرازٕ	Lord of Death
yala:j (m.)	یلاج	treatment
yal d'un (v)	یلِ دیُن	to shrug
yavI (ad)	یوٕ	the day before yesterday
yaslI (ad)	یسلہٕ	often, fully
yahsa:s kamtari: (f.)	یحساس کمتری	inferiority complex
ya: (c.)	یا	either, or
yA:j (f.s.)	یآج	a kind of saltish cake *ya:ji* (p.)
ya:d (f.s.)	یادِ	memory
ya:math (ad)	یامتھ	as soon as
ya:r (m.)	یار	friend
ya:ra:nI (m.)	یارانہٕ	friendship
ya:rbal (m.)	یاربل	river bank
ya:ri kul (m.s.)	یارِ کُل	pine tree *ya:ri kul'* (p)
ya:r ba:sh (a)	یارباش	friendly
ya:l (m.)	یال	hair of horse
ya:vI (a)	یاوٕ	handsome, beautiful
ya:vun (m.)	یاوُن	youth
ya:sha: (ad)	یاشا	suddenly

yi (pr.m.s.)	یہ	this *yim* (p) *yi* (pr.f.s.) *yimI* (p)
yikIvaTI (ad)	یکہ وٹہ	at a time, together
yija:bath (f.)	یجابتھ	pre-marriage ceremony in Muslims
yitimina:n	یتمنان	leisure, confidence
yitimina:nI sa:n (ad)	یتمنانہ سان	with confidence
yithI tithI (ad)	یتھہ تتھہ	somehow or other
yithay h'uv (ad)	یتھے ہیو	sad
yida:rI (m.)	یدارٕ/ادارٕ	institution
yinIvo:l vakhIt (m.)	ینہ وول وقت	future, coming events
yinaspekTar (m.)	ینسپکٹر/انسپکٹر	inspector
yinjan (m.)	ینجن/انجن	road roller, engine
yintika:l (m.)	ینتقال/انتقال	death, mutation
yintikha:b (m.)	ینتخاب/انتخاب	extract, election, revenue record
yintiza:m (m.)	ینتظام/انتظام	arrangement
yibli:s (m.s.)	یبلیس	the devil
yiba:datga:h (m.)	عبادتگاہ	place of worship for Muslims
yibtida: (m.)	ابتدا	beginning
yimtiha:n (m.)	امتحان	examination
yirIvun (v.m.s.)	یرٕوُن	floating *yirIvIn'* (m.p.f.s.) *yirIvIni* (f.p.)
yirIvIn' na:v (f.)	یرٕوٕنۍ ناو	floating boat, confusion
yilA:hi: (f.)	یلاہی	my God, heavenly, O God
yivInuk (a.m.s.)	یوٕنُک	first born issue *yivInIk'* (p) *yivInIc* (f.s.) *yivInIci* (f.p.)
yihAy (ad)	یہَے	this very
yija:d (m.)	یجاد/ایجاد	invention
yi:t' (ad)	ییتۍ	as many
yi:d (f.)	عید	Id - a Muslim festival
yi:ma:nda:r (a)	یماندار/ایماندار	honest
yi:sA:y (m.)	ییساے/عسائی	Christian
yija:zath (m.)	یجازت/اجازت	permission
yeti (ad)	یٚتہِ	here (locational)
yet'an (ad)	یٚتین	here (locational)
yetinas (ad)	یٚتہِ نس	here (locational)
yetiyo:r (ad)	یٚتہِ یور	from now onwards
yembIrzal (f.)	یمبرزل	narcissus
yemipatI (ad)	یٚمہِ پتہ	after this
yemi bro~h (ad)	یٚمہِ برونٛہہ	before this
yemi vAriyi (ad)	یٚمہِ ؤرِیہِ	this year
yemi sa:tI (ad)	یٚمہِ ساتہ	at whichever time
yelI (a)	یٚلہ	open

yeli (ad)	ییٚلہِ	when
yehsa:n (m.)	ییٚحسان/احسان	favour
ye:za:r (m.)	ییٚزار	tousers
ye:r (m.)	ییٚر	wool
ye:run (vi.)	ییٚرُن	arrange thread cover for weaving
ye:l anun (v)	ییٚل انُن	to subdue
yi:run (vi.)	ییٖرُن	to float
yi:rIna:vun (vc.)	ییٖرٕناوُن	to cause to float
yuth (ad)	یُتھ	like this, this type of
yuthuy (ad)	یُتھُے	as soon as
yus (pr.m.s.)	یُس	who, which one *yim* (m.p.) *y>sI* (f.s.) *yimI* (f.p.)
yun (v.m.s.)	یُن	to come *yin'* (m.p.,f.s.) *yini* (f.p.)
yu:p (m.)	یوٗپ	flood
yot (ad)	یوٚت	here
yot ta:m (ad)	یوٚت تام	upto this point
yodIvay (ad)	یوٚدٕوَے	although, even if
yo:kun (ad)	یوکُن	to this side
yo:ni (f.)	یونہِ	sacred thread
yo:r (ad)	یور	here (directional)
yo:rkun (ad)	یورکُن	to this direction
y>khti: (f.)	یوٚکھتی	power, way
y>d (m.)	یوٚد	battle, war

r

rIkh (f.s.)	رٕکھ	line *rIkhI* (p)
rIsh (f.)	رٕش	jealousy, hatred
rIshun (v)	رٕشُن	to like
rIDun (vi.)	رٕڈُن	to persist, to be persistent
rInun (vi.)	رٕنُن	wear with use, be worn out
rAtandi:p (m.)	رَتن دیپ	the sacred lamp
rAph'gor (m.s.)	رَفہٕ گوٗر	darner *rAph'gAr'* (p)
rAmb' (f.s.)	رَمب	an agricultural instrument *rambi* (p)
rAsi:d (m.)	رَسید	receipt
rAs'ul (a)	رَسیُل	juicy
rAham dil (a)	رَحم دِل	kind hearted
rA:Th (f.p.)	رٲٹھ	creepers *ra:Th* (s)
rA:Thva~:gun (m.s.)	رٲٹھ وانٛگُن	tomato *rA:Thva~:gan* (p)
rA~:D' (m.)	رانٛڈ	ring leader, head strong
rAph' kA:m (f.)	رَفہٕ کٲم	darning
rA:say (ad)	رٲسے	slowly
rakh (f.s.)	رَکھ	thick forest *rakhI* (p)
rakhIt (m.)	رَخت	dress

rag (f.s.)	رگ	vein *ragI* (p)
ratsh (ad)	رژھ	a little
ranzIna:vun (vt.)	رنزناوُن	to please
raz (f.s.)	رز	rope *razI* (p)
raza:mand (m.)	رضامند	agreed
razA:y (f.s.)	رزٲے	quilt *raza:yi* (p)
raTIna:vun (v.m.s.)	رٹناوُن	to get someone caught/ arrested *raTIna:vIn'* (m.p.,f.s.) *raTIna:vIni* (f.p.)
raTun (v.m.s.)	رٹُن	to catch, to hold *raTIn'* (m.p.,f.s.) *raTIni* (f.p.)
ratI tsu:r (m.)	رتہٕ ژوٗر	black motion - a disease
rath (m.)	رتھ	blood
ranIna:vun (vc.m.s.)	رنہٕ ناوُن	to get cooked *ranIna:vIn'* (m.p.,f.s.) *ranIna:vIni* (f.p.)
ranun (v.m.s.)	رنُن	to cook *ranIn'* (m.p.,f.s.) *ranIni* (f.p.)
rang (m.)	رنگ	colour
rangun	رنگُن	to colour, dye, sycophancy
rangIda:r (ad)	رنگہٕ دار	coloured
rangItsAr (f.s.)	رنگہٕ ژٔر	kingfisher, a bird *rangItsari* (p)
rangur (m.s.)	رنگُر	dyer *rangIr'* (p)
randI (m.)	رندہٕ	plane
rang sa:z (m.)	رنگ ساز	dyer
rapha:kat (m.)	رفاقت	help
raphal (m.)	رفل	a type of woollen cloth
rabar (m.)	ربر	rubber
raba:bI (m.)	ربابہٕ	a musical instrument
rabar bo:tal (m.)	ربر بوتل	hot water bottle
rala:vun (v.m.s.)	رلاوُن	to add, to mix, to join*rala:vIn'* (m.p.,f.s.) *rala:vIni* (f.p.)
ralun (v.m.s.)	رلُن	to resemble, to mix up *ralIn'* (m.p.,f.s.) *ralIni* (f.p.)
rachun (vi.)	رچھُن	to protect
rav zav (v)	روزو	coming and going
rash (v)	رش	rush
rashvI (m.)	رشوٕ	bribe
rashvatkhor (a)	رشوت خور	corrupt, one who accepts bribe
rashvatkh>ri: (f.)	رشوت خوٚری	corruption
ras (m.)	رس	gravy, juice
rasIm (m.)	رسم	custom
rasI rasI (ad)	رسہ رسہ	slowly

rasu:l (m.)	رسوٗل	prophet
raso:y (m.)	رسوے	kitchen
rasmulkhat (m.)	رسم الخط	script
rahanuma: (m.)	رہنما	guide, leader
rahan sahan (m.)	رہن سہن	way of life, living
ratshrun (vt.)	رٔژھرُن	to save, good relations
ra:z (m.)	راز	secret
ra:zI (m.)	رازٕ	king
ra:zIhA~:z (m.)	رازٕ ہانٛز	swan, goose
ra:zI p>thIr (m.)	رازٕ پوتھٕر	prince
ra:zI ku:r	رازٕ کوٗر	princess
ra:zma:h (m.)	رازٕ ماہ	kidney beans
ra:zma:h hemI (m.)	رازٕ ماہ ہیمہ	green kidney beans
ra:tIkrI:l (m.)	راتہٕ کرٛیل	bat/bats
ra:tImogul (m.s.)	راتہٕ موگل	owl *ra:tImogal* (p)
ra:th (ad)	راتھ	yesterday
ra:th (f.s.)	راتھ	night *rA:ts* (p)
ra:d (m.)	راد	size, length
ra:th k'ut (m.)	راتھ کیٚت	in the night
ra:n (f.m.s.)	ران	thigh *ra:nI* (p)
ra:mIhu:n (m.s.)	رامہٕ ہوٗن	wolf *ra:mIhu:n'* (p)

ra:mInavam (f.)	رامہٕ نوم	Ramanavmi, Lord Rama's birth day
ra:mra:mb AdrIn'du:n' (f.)	رامہ رامہ بٔڈرِ دوٗنۍ	rainbow
ra:vun (v.m.s.)	راوُن	to be lost *ra:vIn'* (m.p.,f.s.) *ra:vIni* (f.p.)
ra:vIra:vun (v.m.s.)	راوِراوُن	to lose *ra:vIra:vIn'* (m.p.,f.s.) *ra:vIra:vIni* (f.p.)
ra:shan (m.)	راشن	ration
rika:D (m.)	ریکاڑ	record
rikib (f.)	رِکیب	small dish, plate
rindI (a)	رِنٛدٕ	beautiful
riya:yath (f.)	رِیایتھ	concession
reya:sat (m.)	ریاست	state
risI (m.)	رِسیہ	recess
risA:rIc (m.)	ریسٔرچ	research
risa:lI (m.)	رسالہ	magazine
ristI (m.)	رِستہ	a meat dish
rih (m.)	رِہ	rheumatism, arthritis
rivun (vi.)	رِوُن	to cry
ri~:Th (f.)	رینٛٹھ	constant weeping
ri:th (f.)	ریٖتھ	tradition
ri:ma:Th (m.)	ریماٹھ	beating
ri:shim (f.)	ریشِم	silk
ri:shim k'om (m.s.)	ریشِم کیوم	silk worm *ri:shim kem'* (p)

rekI ADij (f.s.)	ریکہٕ اڈِج	pelvic bone, backbone *rekI ADiji* (p)
rekh (m.)	ریکھ	bird dropping *rekI* (p)
retsh (a)	ریٚژھ	nick name, reproach
retIko:l (m.)	ریتہٕ کول	summer
reth (m.)	ریتھ	month
rey (f.)	ریٚے	ant
reyi o:l (m.)	ریٚے اول	ant hill *reyi A:l'* (p)
reva:j (m.)	ریواج	custom
reva:yath (f.s.)	ریوایتھ	custom, tradition *reva:yatsI* (p)
re:zI (m.)	ریزٕ	pieces
re:zar (m.)	ریزر	blade
re~:zal (m.)	رینزل	guard, one who uses a catapult
re:zga:r (m.)	ریزگار	change, small coins
re:DIvo:l (m.s.)	ریڈٕوول	cart puller *re:DIvA:l'* (p)
re:Diyo: (m.)	ریڈیو	radio
re:Diyo: siTe:shan (m.)	ریڈیو سٹیشن	radio station
re:sh (f.)	ریش	beard
rukun (v.m.s.)	رُکُن	to stop *rukIn'* (m.p.,f.s.) *rukIni* (f.p.)
ruka:vaTh (f.s.)	رُکاوَٹھ	obstacle *ruka:vaTI* (p)
rugA:l' (f.s.)	رُگال	rag *ruga:li* (p)
rut (a.m.s.)	رُت	good *rIt'* (p) *rIts* (f.s.) *rItsI* (f.p.)
ru:d (m.)	روٗد	rain
rum (f.)	رم	crack
ruma:h (m.)	رُماہ	cow pea
ruvIna:vun (v.m.s.)	رُوِناوُن	to get planted *ruvIna:vIn'* (m.p.,f.s.) *ruvIna:vIni* (f.p.)
ruvun (v.m.s.)	رُوُن	to plant *ruvIn'* (m.p.,f.s.) *ruvIni* (f.p.)
ruva~:gan (m.)	رُوانگن	tomato
ruh (m.)	روح	soul
ruhja:n (m)	رُحجان	bent of mind
ru:g (m.)	روٗگ	disease
ru:dIgaTIka:r (m.)	روٗدِ گٹہٕ کار	heavy rainfall
ru:dI jAr' (f.)	روٗدِ جٔر	stream of rain
ru:dI d>h (m.)	روٗدِ دۄہ	rainy day
ru:n (m.s.)	روٗن	husband *rI:n'* (p)
ru:p (a)	روٗپ	beauty
ru:s (m.)	روٗس	Russia
ru:si: (m.)	روٗسی	Russian
ru:s'kAT (f.s.)	روٗسۍ کٔٹ	she deer *ru:s' kaci* (p) *ru:s' koT* (m.s.) *ru:s' kAT'* (m.p.)

ru:hA:ni: (a)	رۄحٲنی	spiritual
rokbI (m.)	رقبہ	area
roT (m.)	رۄٹ	help
rosu:kh (m.)	رۄسوٗخ	influence
ro~:kh (m.)	رۄنٛکھ	thigh
ro:ganjo:sh (m.)	روغن جوش	a mutton preparation
ro:ch (m.s.)	روچھ	guard, watchman *rA:ch'* (p)
ro:zI (m.)	روزٕ	fast kept by Muslims
ro:zdar (m.)	روزدار	one who keeps fast in Ramzan
ro:zun (v.m.s.)	روزُن	to live, to stay *ro:zIn'* (m.p.,f.s.) *ro:zIni* (f.p.)
ro:zmarI (a)	روزمرٕ	daily routine
ro:DI (m.)	روڑٕ	pebbles
ro:n~d (m.)	رونٛد	police on petrol, guard duty
ro:l (m.)	رول	role
ro:shun (vi.)	روشُن	be angry
ro:shanda:n (m.)	روشن دان	ventilator
ro:shan khaya:l (a)	روشن خیال	broad minded
r>kI (m.)	رۄقہ	letter, document
r>ng (m.)	رۄنٛگ	clove, nose pin
r>ni (f.p.)	رۄنہِ	bells
r>tbI (m.)	رۄتبہ	position
r>pay (f.s.)	رۄپےٚ	one rupee *rpIyi* (p)
r>ph (m.)	رۄپھ	silver
r>y (m.)	رۄے	face

l

lIch (f.s.)	لِچھ	nit *lIchi* (p)
lAkIr (f.)	لٔکٕر	wood, timber
lAgIn (m.)	لگٕن	marriage ceremony
lAT' ta:rukh (m.s.)	لٔٹ ٹارُکھ	comet
lAT' va:l (m.)	لٔٹ وال	hair of the tail
lATh'kIj (f.s.)	لٔٹھِکٕج	*guli*, a piece of stick
lATh'kij loTh (m.)	لٔٹھِکِج لوٹھ	tip-cat, guli:-DanDa:
lADkI (m.)	لڑکہ	boy/boys
lADki: (f.s.)	لڑکی	girl *lADkiyi* (p)
lADi:sha:h (m.)	لڑی شاہ	folk singer
lAnD (ad)	لنٛڈ	lame (woman) *lanji* (p)
lAr (f.s.)	لر	house *lari* (p)
lAsh (f.)	لش	torch, a kind of wood used for lighting purpose
lAs' (m.)	لسی	buttermilk
lAhar (m.)	لہر	tuning, wave
lA~:tsh (m.)	لانٛژھ	eunuch
lA:zim (ad)	لازم	important
lA:Th' (f.s.)	لاٹھی	la:Thi:, a stick *la:Thi* (p)

lA:n (f.)	لاَن	line
lA:r (m.)	لاَر	cucumber
lA:v (a.f.s.)	لاَو	delicate *la:vi* (p)
lA:sh (f.s.)	لاَش	big cat *la:shi* (p)
laga:vun (v.m.s.)	لگاوُن	to apply *laga:vIn'* (m.p.,f.s.) *laga:vIni* (f.p.)
labun (vi.)	لبُن	to find
lagun (v.m.s.)	لگُن	suffer pain, to be hurt *lagIn'* (m.p.,f.s.) *lagIni* (f.p.)
lach (ad)	لَچھ	one lac
lachIno:v (n)	لچھِ نوو	God - having many. names
lachi bAd' (m.)	لچھِ بٔڑۍ	lacs of
latsh (f.)	لٔژھ	dust
latshul (m.s.)	لٔژھُل	broom *latshIl'* (p)
l: shIji kul (m.s.)	لژھجہِ کُل	broom plant *latshIji kul'* (p) *latshIj* (f.s.)
lazath (m.s.)	لزَتھ	taste
laDA:y (f.)	لڑاے	quarrel, battle
laTa:vun (v.m.s.)	لٹاوُن	to run away *laTa:vIn'* (m.p.,f.s.) *laTa:vIni* (f.p.)
laThI (m.)	لٹھ	a type of cloth
laDa:yigor (a.m.)	لڑایہِ گور	quarrelsome *laDa:yigAr'* (p) *laDa:yigAr* (f.s.) *laDa:yigari* (f.p.)
lati:phI (m.)	لطیفہٕ	joke
lath (f.)	لَتھ	kick
laDun (vi)	لڑُن	fight
ladun (vt.m.s.)	لدُن	to fill,send,raise *ladIn'* (m.p.,f.s.) *ladIni* (f.p.)
lang (m.)	لنگ	thigh
lang (m.)	لنگ	branch of a tree
langun (vi.)	لنگُن	limp, be lame
lab (f.s.)	لَب	wall *labI* (p)
lam (m.s.)	لَم	a hill slope, mound
lamIna:vun (vc.m.s.)	لمہٕ ناوُن	to get pulled *lamIna:vIn'* (m.p.,f.s.) *lamIna:vIni* (f.p.)
lamun (vi.)	لمُن	to drag,pull,row *lamIn'* (m.p.,f.s.) *lamIni* (f.p.)
lambarda:r (m.)	لمبردار	village head man
lamp (m.)	لیمپ	lamp
lay (f.)	لۓ	tune
lasun (vi.)	لسُن	live long
lasun basun (v)	لسُن بسُن	way of living, living
lal (f.)	لَل	lap
lav (m.)	لو	hay
lavun (vi.m.s.)	لوُن	be worth, to cost *lavIn'* (m.p.,f.s.) *lavIni* (f.p.)

lashkar (m.)	لشکر	military, army, armed forces
la:kam (f.s.)	لاکم	reins, bridle
la:gun (v.m.s.)	لاگُن	to apply, to imitate, to place, to cultivate *la:gIn'* (m.p.,f.s.) *la:gIni* (f.p.)
la~:z (m.s.)	لانٛز	a long stick
la:ng (f.s.)	لانٛگ	a long log
l'a:Th (f.s.)	لیاٹھ	penis (of an adult man)
la:parva:h (a)	لاپرواہ	careless
la:b	لاب	profit
la:maha:l (m.)	لامحال	in any case
la:yi (f.p.)	لایہٖ	pop corn
la:yakh (a)	لایق	good, appropriate
la:yun (vt.)	لایُن	to strike
la:yun (v.m.s.)	لایُن	to beat *la:yIn'* (m.p.,f.s.) *la:yIni* (f.p.)
la:run (v.m.s.)	لارُن	to run, to follow *la:rIn'* (m.p.,f.s.) *la:rIni* (f.p.)
la:l (m.s.)	لال	pupil of an eye
la:lIc (m.)	لالِچ	greed, attraction, temptation
la:lIphol (m.)	لالٕپھول	pupil of eye, diamond, dear one
la:lTi:n (m.)	لالٹین	lantern
la:sh (f.s.)	لاش	dead body, corpse *la:shI* (p)
likhA:y (f.s.)	لِکھاے	writing
likhA:r' (m.)	لِکھاری	writer
liTar (m.)	لِٹر	litre
litIr (f.s.)	لِتر	.saw blade *litIri* (p)
lithvun (v.m.s.)	لِتھوُن	to drag (in mud) *lithvIn'* (m.p.,f.s.) *lithIvIni* (f.p.)
lithIna:vun (vt.)	لِتھناوُن	to drag
lin' (a. f.s.)	لِنی	slippery
livan (f.s.)	لِوَن	spade *livIni* (p)
livun (vi)	لِوُن	to mop,plaster
lisI (a)	لِسہٕ	weak, frail
liba:s (m.)	لِباس	dress
li:la: (f.)	لیلا	bhajan, a devotional song
li:sI (f.)	لیسہٕ	a kind of vegetable
lej' (f.s.)	لیجۍ	earthen utencil *leji* (p)
ledIr (f.)	لیدر	turmeric
ledur (a)	لیدُر	yellow coloured *ledIr'* (a.p.)
lekcar (m.)	لیکچر	lecture
levun (v.m.s.)	لیوُن	to lick *levIn'* (m.p.,f.s.) *levIni* (f.p.)
le:kin (c)	لیکن	but

le:khIna:vun (vc.m.s.)	لیکھناوُن	to make someone write *le:khIna:vIn'* (m.p.,f.s.) *le:khIna:vIni* (f.p.)
le:khun (vt.m.s.)	لیکھُن	to write *le:khIn'* (m.p.,f.s.) *le:khIni* (f.p.)
le:n de:n (m.)	لین دین	transaction
le:ph (f.)	لیف	quilt
lutuph (m.)	لُطف	pleasure, enjoyment
lurIpa:rI (m.)	لُرپار	destruction
lu:kI adab (m.)	لۆکہ اَدب	folk literature
lu:kI g'avun (m.s.)	لۆکہ گیوُن	folk songs
lu:kh (m.p.)	لۆکھ	people
lu~:g' (m.)l	لۆنگی	adies cloth belt
lu:b (m.)	لۆب	greed, attraction
lu:bIvun (a)	لۆبہ وُن	pleasing, attractive
lu:r (f.s.)	لۆر	stick *lo:ri* (p)
lu:Tun (vi.)	لۆٹُن	to plunder
loT (m.)	لۆٹ	tail *lAT'* (p)
loTh (m.s.)	لۆٹھ	a stick *lATh'* (p)
loD (m.s.)	لۆڈ	sweet ball *lAD'* (p)
lot lot (ad)	لوتہٕ لوتہٕ	slowly
l>ti l>ti (ad)		slowly
long (ad.m.s.)	لۆنگ	lame *lAng'* (p)
lAnD (f.s.)	لَنڈ	branch of a tree *lanji* (p)
longun (m.)	لۆنگُن	local wooden measurement pot for about 2 Kgs
lobkun (ad)	لۆبکُن	aside
lo:ch (m.s.)	لوچ	woollen matted cloth, a woollen pheran *lA:ch'* (p)
lo:nun (v.m.s.)	لونُن	to harvest *lo:nIn'* (m.p.,f.s.) *lo:nIni* (f.p.)
lo:l (m.)	لول	love, affection
lo:v (m.s.)	لوو	delicate *lA:v'* (p)
lo:s (f.s.)	لوس	earthworm, lying in woman *lo:sI* (p)
lo:sun (v)	لوسُن	to set, to disappear
lo:sun (vi.)	لوسُن	be weary, setting of sun
lo:nun (vt.)	لوانُن	to reap
l>tun (vi.)	لوتُن	be light
l>kuT (a.m.s.)	لوکُٹ	young, small *lkIT'* (p) *lkIT* (f.s.) *lkIci* (f.p.)
l>kTun (v.m.s.)	لوکٹُن	to become young/small *l>kTIn'* (m.p.,f.s.) *l>kTIni* (f.p.)
l>ga:th (f.)	لوغاتھ	dictionary
l>bur (m.s.)	لوبُر	cow dung cake *l>bar* (p)

l>y (f.)	لوے	bronze
l>rI (a)	لوٗرِ	immatured, easy go lucky
lkIca:r (m.)	لوکچار	childhood

V

vIshkI (f.)	وِشکہ	barley
vIhIr' vAriyas (ad)	وِہرۍ وۄریس	throughout the year
vAkish (f.)	وۄکیش	eagerness, lust, restlessness
vAki:l (m.)	وۄکیل	lawyer
vAzi:r (m.)	وۄزیر	minister
vAzi:r A:la: (m.)	وۄزیر اعلیٰ	chief minister
vAnIpo:sh (m.)	وَنہٕ پوش	wild flower
vAr (f.)	وۄر	beaten rice with salt, stew
vAri: (m.)	وۄری	year
vAl' vAl' (ad)	وۄلۍ وۄلۍ	quickly
vAhra:th (f.s.)	وُہراتھ	rainy season *vAhrA:ts* (p)
vAhrvA:r (f.)	وُہرواٰر	first death anniversary
vA:kIph (a)	واٰقِف	acquainted
vA:kphiyat (f.)	واٰقفیت	knowledge, acquaintance
vA~:kh (f.s.)	واٰنکھ	coTi, tassel *vA~:kI* (p)
vA:j (f.s.)	واٰج	ring *va:ji* (p)
vA:jib (ad)	واٰجِب	proper
vA:di: (f.)	واٰدی	valley
vA:r (f.)	واٰر	an earthen pot
vA:r (f.)	واٰر	kitchen garden
vA:r (m.)	واٰر	enemity
vA:r' (f.)	واٰرۍ	turn
vA:ra:g (m.)	واٰراگ	indifference, apathy
vA:ra:n (a)	واٰران	deserted
vA:r'uv (m.)	واٰرِیو	husband's home
vA:rishin' (a.f.)	واٰرِشِنۍ	one year old (girl child)
vA:rishun (a.m.)	واٰرِشُن	one year old (baby boy)
vA:l'vin' (a.f.s.)	واٰلِوِنۍ	pregnant (animal) *vA:l' vini* (p)
vakhtI vakhtI (ad)	وقتہٕ وقتہٕ	at times
vaka:nI (m.)	وکانہٕ	something wrong
vakur phirun (v)	وکُر پھِرُن	volt face
vakhray (ad)	وکھرے	separately
vakh/vakhIt (m.)	وق/وقتہٕ	time
vakhnay (f.)	وکھنے	explanation
vagIv' gor (m.)	وگوِ گور	mat maker *vagIv' gAr'* (p)
vaguv (m.s.)	وگوٗ	straw mat *vagIv'* (p)
vach (m.)	وچھ	chest
vatshIr (f.s.)	وٕژھر	she calf *vatshri* (p)

vetshIna:vun (v.m.s.)	ویٚژھناوُن	carding *vetshIna:vIn'* (m.p.,f.s.) *vetshIna:vIni* (f.p.)
vajah (m.)	وَجہ	reason
vazun (vi.)	وَزُن	sound of a musical instrument *vazIn'* (m.p.,f.s.) *vazIni* (f.p.)
vazan (m.)	وَزَن	weight
vaTun (v.m.s.)	وَٹُن	to close *vaTIn'* (m.p.,f.s.) *vaTIni* (f.p.)
vazA:h (ad)	وَزاہ	show off, stylish
vaTukh (m.)	وَٹُکھ	all the utencils put together used for worship on Shivaratri by Kashmiri Hindus
vatan (m.)	وَطن	country
vath (f.s.)	وَتھ	road *vatI* (p)
vathIra:vun (vi.m.s.)	وَتھٕراوُن	to lay down (like a bed) *vathIra:vIn'* (m.p.,f.s.) *vathIra:vIni* (f.p.)
vathrun (m.)	وَتھرُن	bedding
vadIna:vun (vc.m.s.)	وَدٕناوُن	to make someone cry *vadIna:vIn'* (m.p.,f.s.) *vadIna:vIni* (f.p.)
vadav (f.)	ودو	blessings
vadun (v)	ودُن	to cry, to weep
vadIvun (a.)	ودوُن	one who weeps, weepy *vadIvIn'* (m.p.,f.s.) *vadIvIni* (f.p.)
van (m.)	وَن	forest
vanIna:vun (vc.m.s.)	وٕنہٕ ناوُن	to make someone say, ladies singing *vanIna:vIn'* (m.p.,f.s.) *vanIna:vIni* (f.p.)
vanİvun (m.)	وٕنہٕ وُن	marriage folk songs
vanun (vi.m.s.)	وَنُن	tell, to speak, say *vanIn'* (m.p.,f.s.) *vanIni* (f.p.)
vanIvun/ vanIna:vun (vi.)	وٕنہٕ وُن / وٕنہٕ ناوُن	to sing in chorus (by women)
van kkur (m.)	وٕنہٕ کوکُر	wild turky, wild cock
vandI (m.)	وَنٛدٕ	winter season
vayun (vi.)	وَیُن	be suitable in eating, to suit
valun (vi.)	وَلُن	wrap, cover, dress oneself
vavun (vt.)	وَوُن	to sow
vasun (vi.)	وَسُن	to come down, descend
vendun (v.m.s.)	ویٚنٛدُن	to sacrifice *vendIn'* (m.p.,f.s.) *vendIni* (f.p.)
vanbro:r (m.s.)	وٕنہٕ برور	wild cat *van brA:r'* (p)
vanhA:r (f.)	وٕنہٕ ہار	wild maina, beautiful woman
vapha:dA:ri: (f.)	وفاداری	faithfulness

vapha:da:r (a)	وفادار	faithful
vaba: (f.)	وبا	epidemic
vayakh (m.)	ویکھ	Vaishak-name of the first month of Bikrami era
vayknTh (m.)	ویکنٹھ	paradise
var (m.)	ور	twist
varA:y (pp.)	ورائے	without
varaksha:p (m.)	ورکشاپ	workshop
varibatI (m.)	وربتہ	spiced food
vara:sat (f.)	وراثت	hereditary property
varukh (m.)	ورق	sheet of paper, Page
varus (m.)	ورس	anniversary, festival
varta:vun (v)	ورتاوُن	to behave, to use
vardan (m.)	وَردن	wedding dress
vardi: (f.)	وردی	uniform (dress)
vala:han	ولاہن	oath, by God
valun (v.m.s.)	ولُن	to wrap *vallIn'* (m.p.,f.s.) *vallIni* (f.p.)
vavun (v.m.s.)	ووُن	to sow *vavIn'* (m.p.,f.s.) *vavIni* (f.p.)
vashnav (m.s.)	وشنو	vegetarian *vashnAv'* (p)
vas (m.f.)	وَس	marrow
vasal (m.)	وصوَل	union of lovers
vaise: (adv.)	ویسے	as a matter of fact

vasi:yat (f.)	وصیت	will
vasi:yatna:mI (m.)	وصیت نامہ	will deed
vasun (v.m.s.)	وسُن	to come down *vasIn'* (m.p.,f.s.) *vasIni* (f.p.)
vasva:s (m.)	وسواس	lurking fear, apprehension
vaham (m.)	وہم	doubt, misgiving
va:ka:h (m.)	واقع	incident
v'a:kul (a.)	ویاکل	anxious, perplexed, restless
v'a:kran (m.)	ویاکرن	grammar
va:kh (m.)	واکھ	verses of Lal Ded or any other saint
va~:gIj vo:r (m.)	وانگج وور	rented house
va:z (m.)	واز	sermon
va:zI (m.)	وازہ	cook
va:Tun (vt.m.s.)	واٹُن	to unite, fix *va:TIn'* (m.p.,f.s.) *va:TIni* (f.p.)
va:TIna:vun (vc.m.s.)	واٹہٕ ناوُن	to get fixed *va:TIna:vIn'* (m.p.,f.s.) *va:TIna:vIni* (f.p.)
va:tIj (f.s.)	واتج	woman sweeper *va:tIji* (p)
va:Th (m.)	واٹھ	joint, relation
va:tul (m.s.)	واتل	shoemaker, sweeper *va:tal* (p)
va~:dur (m.)	واندر	monkey *va~:dar* (p)

va:n (m.)	وان	shop
va~:gun (m.)	وانٛگُن	brinjal *va~:gan* (p)
va:nI thar (f.)	وانۍ تھَر	varandah of a shop
va:y (i)	وائے	alas
va:yun (v.m.s.)	وایُن	to play on musical instrument *va:yIn'* (m.p.,f.s.) *va:yIni* (f.p.)
va:ren' (f.)	وارێنۍ	midwife
va:rI ka:rI (ad)	وارِ کارِ	well, all right
va:rI va:rI (ad)	وارِ وارِ	slowly
va:D (m.)	واڑ	ward
va:l (m.)	وال	hair
va:lun (vt.m.s.)	والُن	to bring down, pluck, descend *va:lIn'* (m.p.,f.s.) *va:lIni* (f.p.)
va:li:ba:l (f.)	والی بال	volley ball
va:v (m.)	واو	wind
va:vIj (f.s.)	واوِج	hand fan *va:vIji* (p)
va:vIpet' (m.)	واوِ پێٹۍ	chicken pox
va:sh kaDun (v)	واش کڈُن	to straighten
va:h va:h (i)	واہ واہ	expression of happiness or appreciation
va:skaTh (m.)	واسکَٹھ	jacket
va:hara:vun (v.m.s.)	واہراوُن	to stretch, to spread *va:hra:vIn'* (m.p.,f.s.) *va:hra:vIni* (f.p.)
va:hrun/ va:hra:vun (vt.)	واہرُن / واہراوُن	to spread out
vizi vizi (ad)	وِزِ وِزِ	at times
viziTar (m.)	وِزِٹَر	visitor
vidur (m.)	وِدُر	widower
viz (ad)	وِز	moment, time
vishva:s (m.)	وِشواس	belief
vi:rk'om (m.)	ویرکیوم	colchicum luteum
vi:rikul (m.s.)	ویرِکُل	salin, willow tree
veglun (vi.)	ویگلُن	to melt
vekhut (a.m.s.)	ویکھُت	terrific, strange *vekhIt'* (m.p.) *vekhIts* (f.s.) *vekhItsi* (f.p.)
vetsa:run (v.m.s.)	ویژارُن	to think, to ponder over *vetsa:rIn'* (m.p.,f.s.) *vetsa:rIni* (f.p.)
vetshIra:vun (vt.)	ویژھراوُن	carding
veThIra:vun (vi.)	ویٹھراوُن	make fat
vepra:vun (vi.)	ویپراوُن	cause to pervade
vAzi:phI (m.)	وظیفہٕ	scholarship
veThun (v.m.s.)	ویٹھُن	to become fat, fatter *veThIn'* (m.p.,f.s.) *veThIni* (f.p.)
veth (f.)	ویتھ	the Jehlum
vedva:n (m.)	ویدوان	scholar
ves (f.s.)	ویس	a girl's girl friend *vesI* (p)

vugrI (m.)	وُگرٕ	cooked beaten rice
vuchun (v.m.s.)	وُچھُن	to see *vuchIn'* (m.p.,f.s.) *vuchIni* (f.p.)
vuchan vo:l (m.s.)	وُچھن وول	spectator *vuchan vA:l'* (p)
vuz (m.s.)	وُز	corridor
vuzun (v.m.s.)	وُزُن	to spring *vuzIn'* (m.p.,f.s.) *vuzIni* (f.p.)
vuzImalI (f.)	وُزِملہٕ	lightening
vuTh (m.)	وُٹھ	lip/lips
vuThun (vt.)	وُٹھُن	to twist
vuDIr (f.)	وُڈٕر	plateau
vuDun (v.m.s.)	وُڈُن	to fly *vuDIn'* (m.p.,f.s.) *vuDIni* (f.p.)
vuDIna:vun (vt.)	وُڈٕناوُن	cause to fly
vuDa:vun (v.m.s.)	وُڈاوُن	to make fly *vuDa:vIn'* (m.p.,f.s.) *vuDa:vIni* (f.p.)
vudI (m)	وُدٕ	a fragrance,. aloe
vunal (f.)	وُنَل	fog, mist
vunun (vt.)	وُنُن	to face bad luck
vunun (v)	وَنُن	to take wrong decision
vun'ukta:m (ad)	وُنیکھ تام	uptil now
vun' (ad)	وُنۍ	just now
vun'kenas (ad)	وُنۍ کِنِس	at present
vun'k'an (ad)	وُنۍ کین	at this particular moment
vupun (vi.)	وُپُن	burn inside
vuphun (vi.)	وُپھُن	to fly
vumIr (f.)	وُمِر	age
vumIr kA:d (m.)	وُمرٕ قاد / عُمر قاد	life imprisonment
vurIbal (m.)	وُرِبل	a huge kitchen
vulTI (a)	وُلٹہٕ	opposite, strange
vushIne:r (m.)	وُشہٕ نیر	warmth
vushIna:vun (v.m.s.)	وُشہٕ ناوُن	to warm *vushIna:vIn'* (m.p.,f.s.) *vushIna:vIni* (f.p.)
vutsun (vi.)	وُژُن	be burnt (of vegetable etc.)
vushun (a)	وُشُن	warm
vushkI (m.)	وُشکہٕ	barley
vushkI kasha:bI (m.)	وُشکہٕ کشابہٕ	barley water
vuh (a)	وُہ	twenty
vuhim (a)	وُہِم	twentieth
vu~:Th (m.)	ووُنٹھ	camel(s)
vu:r (m.)	ووُر	cover
v'okhut (a)	ویوکھُت	dreadful, strange
v>tshab (m.)	ووژھَب	function, festival
votsh (m.s.)	ووژھ	he calf
voT (m.s.)	ووٹ	room on ground floor *vAT'* (p)
voTal k'om (m.s.)	ووٹل کیوم	cockroach *voTal kem'* (p)

v'oTh (a.m.s.)	وۄٹھ	bulky, fat *veTh'* (p) *veTh* (f.s.) *vechi* (f.p.)
v>DIpalav (m.)	وۆڈِپلو	head dress for ladies
vaba:h (m.)	وَباہ	epidemic
vostIha:kh (m.)	ووسۭتہٕ ہاکھ	a green vegetable
vohvun (v)	وۄہوُن	to abuse
vo:T (m.)	ووٹ	vote
vo:n' (m.)	وونی	shopkeeper
vo:nun (v.m.s.)	وونُن	to weave, to knit *vo:nIn'* (m.p.,f.s.) *vo:nIni* (f.p.)
vo:nIna:vun (vc.m.s.)	وونہٕ ناوُن	to get knitted *vo:nIna:vIn'* (m.p.,f.s.) *vo:nIna:vIni* (f.p.)
vo:khI (a)	ووکھ	dangerous, strange
vo:rInecuv (m.s.)	وورِنیچُو	step son *vo:rIneciv'* (p)
vo:rIbo:y (m.s.)	وورِبوے	step brother *vo:rIbA:y* (p)
vo:rIbeni (f.)	وورِبیٚنہٕ	step sister/ step sisters
vo:rI mA:j (f.s.)	وورِ مآج	step mother *vo:rI ma:ji* (p)
vo:vur (m.)	ووۄر	weaver
vo:run (vi.)	وورُن	talk in one's sleep
vo:lun (vi.)	وولُن	be incensed, fly in a rage
vo:hrIvo:d (m.)	ووہرِوود	birthday

vyesrun (vi.)	ویٚسرُن	fall from hand, become fragile
v>gun (a)	وۆگُن	slanting upwards
v>zul (a.m.s.)	وۆزُل	red *v>zIl'* (p) *v>zIj* (f.s.) *v>zIji* (f.p.)
v>zulun (vi.)	وۆزُلُن	become red
v>zIja:r (m.)	وۆزِجار	redness
v>Th (f.s.)	وۆٹھ	jump *v>TI* (p.)
v>thra:vun (vt.)	وۆتھراوُن	wipe clean
v>DInAn' (a.f.s.)	وۆڈِنٕنی	bare headed *v>DInani* (p) *v>DInon* (a.m.s.) *v>DInAn'* (p)
v>tar (m.)	وۆتُر	north
v>tlun (v.m.s.)	وۆتلُن	to rise *v>tlIn'* (m.p.,f.s.) *v>τlIni* (f.p.)
v>thun (v.m.s.)	وۆتھُن	to get up *v>thIn'* (m.p.,f.s.) *v>thIni* (f.p.)
v>thIra:vun (v.m.s.)	وۆتھِراوُن	to wipe out *v>thIra:vIn'* (m.p.,f.s.) *v>thIra:vIni* (f.p.)
v>n' (ad)	وۆنی	now
v>ndI (m.)	وۆنِد	interest
v>pIda:vun (v.m.s.)	وۆپِداوُن	to grow *v>pIda:vIn'* (m.p.,f.s.) *v>pIda:vIni* (f.p.)

v>par (a.m.s.)	ووپر	unknown, stranger
v>prA:zi: (f.)	ووپرآزی	inacquaintance, unfamiliarity
v>pa:y (m.)	ووپاے	way out
v>me:d (f.)	وومید	hope
v>sh (m.)	ووش	deep sigh
v>stI (m.)	ووستہٕ	teacher, artiste
v>sI drsI (n.m.)	ووسہٕ درٕوسہٕ	crowd, hustle and bustle
v>khur (m.s.)	ووکھُر	turn
v>khur d'un (vt.)	ووکھُر دیُن	to turn upside down
vungun (vi.)	وٗنگُن	crying of dogs/jackals

sh

shAthIr (m.)	شٕتھُر	enemy
shA:j (f.s.)	شآج	she jackal *sha:ji* (p)
shA~:ti: (f.)	شانتی	peace
shAstIrdA:ri: (a.)	شستٕردآری	armed person
shA:diya:nI (m.)	شآدِیانہٕ	happy celebration
shA:m' (f.)	شآمہِ	meat dish
shA:yir (n)	شآیر	poet
shA:yri: (f.)	شآیری	poetry
shA:hid (m.)	شآہِد	witness
shA:hi: astabal (m.)	شآہی اَستبل	royal stable
shA:hi: darba:r (m.)	شآہی دربار	royal court
shakII (f.)	شکٕل	shape, picture
shakarkand (m.)	شکرقند	sweet potato
shaka:yath (f.)	شکایتھ	complaint
shakh (m.)	شکھ	doubt
shakhti: (f.)	شکھتی	power
shakhs (m.)	شخص	person
shakhsi: ra:j (f.)	شخصی راج	autocracy
shakhsiyat (f.)	شخصِیتھ	personality
shatIvuh (a)	شترٕوُہ	twentysix
shatra~j (m.)	شطرنج	chess
shath (a)	شتھ	hundred
shada:d (a)	شداد	over clever, mischievous
shaDmo:s (m.)	شڈموس	sixth month of death
shangIr (f.)	شنگرٕ	liquorice
shapha: (m.)	شفاہ	cure, curing power
shapha:kha:nI (m.)	شفاخانہٕ	hospital
shab (f.)	شب	night
shabibara:th (f.)	شبِ براتھ	a religious festival of Muslims
shabikadIr (f.)	شبِ قدر	a festival of Muslims
shabnam (m.)	شبنم	dew

shama:h (m.)	شمع	candle
shar (m.)	شر	desire, yearning, longing
sharIm (f.)	شرم	shame
sharat (m.)	شرط	bet
sharaph (m.)	شرف	value
shara:phat (f.)	شرافت	gentleness
sharA:b' (a)	شرآبی	drunkard
shara:b (m.)	شراب	liquor
shara:rath (f.)	شرارتھ	anger
sharA:yi: ye:za:r (m.)	شرآئی یېزار	a kind of trousers
shari:ph (a)	شریف	gentle
sharbath (f.)	شربتھ	juice
sharmandI (a)	شرمندٕ	ashamed
shalakh (m.)	شلکھ	beating
shav (m.)	شو	human dead body, corpse
shavtsItArdAshi: (f.)	شوژترٕدٔشی	Lord Shiva's day
shavnath (m.)	شوناتھ	Lord Shiva
shahanshA:hi: (m.)	شہنشاہی	monarchy
shahar (m.)	شہر	city
sha:htul (m.)	شاہ تل	mulberry
shAhari: (a)	شٲہری	urban
sha:kh (f.s.)	شاخ	branch of tree *sha:khI* (p)
sha~:t (a)	شانت	peaceful
sha~:d (m.)	شانڈ	pillow
sha~:dIgo~D (m.)	شانڈٕ گونڈ	pillow
sha~:t pA:Th' (ad)	شانت پٲٹھۍ	calmly
sha:d (a)	شاد	happy
sha:n (f.)	شان	grandeur, glory
sha:nI (f.)	شانہٕ	back
sha:nda:r (a)	شاندار	grand
sha:nIboD (a)	شانہٕ بوڈ	respected
sha:ph (m.)	شاف	curse
sha:ba:sh (i)	شاباش	well done
sha:m (m.)	شام	evening
sha:mIpAt' (ad)	شامہٕ پتۍ	after evening
sha:mIrang (a)	شامہٕ رنگ	blackish colour
sha:man bA:g' (ad)	شامن باگ	in the evening
sha:h (m.)	شاہ	breath
sha:math (f.)	شامتھ	ill luck, misfortune
sha:hma:r (m.)	شاہمار	king cobra
sha:l (m.)	شال	jackal
sha:l (m.s.)	شال	shawl
shikas (f.)	شکست	defeat, poverty
shig (f.)	شگ	bad omen
shiThI (a)	شٹھہٕ	strict, a bigot
shiThun (y)	شٹھُن	to be dried up, to dry

shitIl' (f.)	شِتلِہ	small pox
shinya: (m.)	شِنیا	space, ruin
shil (f.)	شِل	spirogyra
shilva:r (f.)	شِلوار	trousers
shiv (m.)	شِو	Shiva
shivli~g (m.)	شِولِنگ	idol of Shiva
shishargA~:T (s) shishargA~:TI (f.p.)	شِشرگانٹھ	icicle
shihul (a.m.s.) shihIl' (p) shihIj (f.s.) shihIji (p)	شِہُل	cool, shade
shi:tal (a)	شیتل	soft minded
shi:th (a)	شیٹھ	eighty
shi:thim (a)	شیٹھِم	eightieth
shi:n (m.)	شین	snow
shi:nIma:n' (f.s.) shi:nIma:ni (p)	شینہٕ مانٛ	lump of snow ice glacier
shi:r'ca:y (f.)	شیرِ چاے	saltish tea with milk
shi:r garIm (a)	شیر گرم	luke warm
shi:shI (m.)	شیشہ	glass, mirror
she (a)	شےٚ	six
shAyitA:ji (a)	شیٚہ تاجی	forty six
shAyitrIh (a)	شیٚہ ترٕہ	thirty six
shAyim (a)	شیٚیم	sixth
sheyishi:th (a)	شیٚہ شیٹھ	eighty six
shari:kh (m.)	شریکھ	partner
shari:ph (a)	شریف	gentle
sheshtIr (m.)	شیشتر	iron
shehja:r (m.)	شہجار	shadow
shehla:vun (vt.m.s.) shehla:vIn' (m.p.,f.s.) shehla:vIni (f.p.)	شیہلاوُن	to make cool
shehlun (vi.m.s.) shehlIn' (m.p.,f.s.) shehlIni (f.p.)	شیہلُن	to be cold
shẹ:ta:n (n)	شیطان	devil, satan
she:run (v.m.s.) she:rIn' (m.p.,f.s.) she:rIni (f.p.)	شیرُن	to repair
she:run tI pA:run (v)	شیرُن تہٕ پارُن	to decorate
she:l (f.) she:lI (p)	شیل	rock
she:v (m.)	شیو	shave
shukriya: (n)	شُکریا	thanks
shuturmurg (m.)	شُترمُرگ	ostritch
shunamath (a)	شُنمتھ	ninetysix
shup (f.)	شُپ	winnowing fan
shup'va:tul (m.)	شُپی واتُل	one who makes winnowing fans
shuma:r (m.)	شُمار	counting, count
shuma:l (f.)	شُمال	north
shur (m.s.) shur' (p)	شُر	child/infant, baby
shura:h (a)	شُراہ	sixteen

shur'gi:	شُرِہگی	childishness
shur'ba:nI (m.)	شُرِبانہٕ	womb
shur'vo:l (m.)	شُرِووٗل	a man having children
shuvanza:h (a)	شُوٕنزاہ	fiftysix
shush (m.s.)	شُش	lungs
shusatath (a)	شُستَتھ	seventy six
shuhA:Th (a)	شُہٲٹھ	sixty six
shuhul (m.)	شُہُل	shadow
shu:bida:r (a)	شوٗبہِ دار	beautiful, graceful, dignified
shu:bun (v.m.s.)	شوٗبُن	to look pleasing/ graceful *shu:bIn'* (m.p.,f.s.) *shu:bIni* (f.p.)
shu:shIno:r (m.)	شوٗشہِ نور	lung
shokIrva:r (f.s.)	شوکہٕ وار	Friday
sh>rbI (m.)	شۄربہٕ	soup
sho:kh (m.)	شوٗخ	desire
sho~:Th (f.)	شوٚنٹھ	ginger
sho:r (n)	شور	noise
sho:rI (m.)	شورٕ	gunpowder
sho:lI (n)	شولہٕ	sparks, flame
sho:lIvun (v)	شولہٕ وُن	blooming, decorative
sh~gun (v)	شوٚنگُن	to sleep
sh>d (a)	شۄد	pure
sh>hrath (f.)	شۄہرَتھ	fame

shrapun (v.m.s.)	شرپُن	digest, to be digested *shrapIn'* (m.p.,f.s.) *shrapIni* (f.p.)
shra:kh (f.s.)	شراکھ	big knife *shra:kI* (p)
shra:n (m.)	شران	bath
shra:nIkuTh (m.s.)	شرانہٕ کُٹھ	bath room *shra:nIkuTh'* (p)
shra:nIpaTh (m.)	شرانہٕ پٹھ	a kind of underwear
shra:puc (m.s.)	شراپُچ	small knife *shra:pIc'* (p)
shra:vun (m.)	شراوُن	Shravan - name of the fourth month of Bikrami era
shru:ts (a)	شروٗژ	pure, clean
shrog (a.m.s.)	شروگ	cheap *shrog'* (p) *shroj* (f.s.) sh>rji (p)
shro:tsun (vi.)	شروژُن	be pure
shr>n' sh>rn (m.)	شرۄنہِ شرۄن	tinkling (of bells)
shru:tsIra:vun (m.s.)	شروٗژہٕ راوُن	to make pure/clean *shru:tsIra:vIn'* (m.p.,f.s.) *shru:tsIra:vIni* (f.p.)

S

sIts (m.)	سِژ	tailor
sItsan (f.s.)	سِژن	needle *sItsni* (p)
sItsI ba:y (f.s.)	سِژہٕ باے	tailor's wife *sItsI ba:yi* (p)

sIthIr (m.)	سِتھٕر	cotton
sIsar (f.)	سِسَر	suffocation, heat
sIh (m.)	سِہہ	lion/lions
sI:th' (pp.)	سٟتۍ	along with
sI:th'vo:l (m.)	سٟتۍ وول	companion, co-traveller
sAtim (a)	سٔتِم	seventh
sAnima: (m.)	سِنیما	cinema
sAn'ts'ath (m.)	سٔنٛژٕتھ	saving
sAdkI (m.)	صٔدقہٕ	charity
sAbi:lI (m.)	سبیٖلہٕ	means
sArkas (m.)	سٔرکَس	circus
sArpin' (f.s.)	سٔرپٕنۍ	snake *sArpini* (p)
sAlkI (m.s.)	سٔلکہٕ	follower
sA:juv (m.s.)	ساجوٕ	wife's sister's husband
sA:D' (f.s.)	ساڑۍ	saree
sA:b (past)	صاب	honorific suffix
sA:yis (m.)	سائیس	horseman, syce
sA:l (m.)	سال	walk
sA:lA:ni: (n)	سالانی	visitor/visitors
sA:sim (a)	ساسِم	thousandth
sagna:vun (vt.)	سگہٕ ناوُن	water (plants)
sakh (ad)	سَخ	hard
sakhti: (f.s.)	سختی	difficulty
sakhrun (vi)	سکھرُن	to get ready, to set forth
sag d'un (vt.)	سگ دِیُن	to water
sajun (v)	سجُن	to be decorated *sajIn'* (m.p.,f.s.) *sajIni* (f.p.)
saja:vun (v.m.s.)	سجاوُن	to decorate *saja:vIn'* (m.p.,f.s.) *saja:vIni* (f.p.)
sazIkul (m.s.)	سزٕکُل	a kind of plant, marsh-mellow
sazIpo:sh (m.)	سزٕپوش	a kind of flower
sazIlong (m.)	سزٕلنگ	a game
s'azar (m.)	سیٛزر	simplicity
sazun (v)	سزُن	to concertrate
saza: (m.)	سزا	punishment
s'aTha: (a)	سیٹھاہ	very much
saDakh (f.s.)	سڑکھ	road *saDIkI* (p)
saDun (v)	سڑُن	to rot
satItA:ji (a)	ستہٕ تاجی	fortyseven
satItrIh (a)	ستہٕ ترٕہ	thirtyseven
satIvanza:h (a)	ستہٕ وُنزاہ	fiftyseven
satIhA:Th (a)	ستہٕ ہاٹھ	sixtyseven
satIthim (a)	ستہٕ تھم	seventieth
satIsatath (a)	ستہٕ ستتھ	seventyseven
satIshi:th (a)	ستہٕ شیٖتھ	eightyseven
satInamath (a)	ستہٕ نمتھ	ninetyseven
satath (a)	سَتتھ	seventy
satut (m.)	سَتُت	hoopoe

sata:vun (v.m.s.)	ستاوُن	to tease *sata:vIn'* (m.p.,f.s.) *sata:vIni* (f.p.)
satrAnD (m.)	ستہٕ رٕنٛڈ	a drudget, cotton carpet
satsang (m.)	ست سنگ	satsang - religious gathering
satra:th (f.)	ست راتھ	a ceremony in Hindu marriage
sath (a)	ستھ	seven
sathzan (m.)	ستھ زن	saint
sath pAd' (m.)	ستھ پٔد	seven-steps ceremony (in marriage)
sath bi:sa:l (a)	ستھ بیسال	hundred and twenty years old, a blessing for long life
sadIr' (f.s.)	سدٕر	waist coat *sadri* (p)
sada: (m.)	صدا	knocking sound
sada:h (m.)	سداہ	seventeen
s'ada:rI (m.)	سیداٗر	fool, moroon
sanI (n)	سنہٕ	era
sanath (f.)	صنتھ	industry
sanad (f.)	صنٛد	certificate
san'ar (m.)	سٔنیر	depth
sangItar (m.)	سنگترٕ	orange
sang (m.)	سنٛگ	association
sangam (m.)	سنگم	confluence, the point where two or more rivers meet
sangarma:lI (f.p.)	سنگرمالہٕ	the range of mountains, dawn
sangi:nI (a)	سنگینہٕ	hard, stiff
sangi marmar (m.)	سنگِ مرمر	marble
sangdil (a)	سنگ دل	stone hearted
sangla:th (a)	سنگلاتھ	hard
sanji:dI (a)	سنجیدٕ	serious
sanji:dIgi: (f.)	سنجیدگی	seriousness
santa:n (m.)	سنتان	child
santu:r (m.)	سنتوٗر	musical instrument
santo:sh (m.)	سنتوش	satisfaction
sand'a: (m.)	سنٛدیا	evening, dusk, evening prayer
sandu:kh (m.)	صندوٗق	box
sanun (v)	سنُن	to go deep
santri: (m.)	سنتری	guard
san'ra:vun (vi.)	سنی راوُن	to make deep
sandra:vun (vi.)	سنٛدراوُن	to light fire
sapun (vi.)	سپُن	be complete, to happen
sapIdun (v.m.s.)	سپدُن	to happen,complete *sapIdIn'* (m.p.,f.s.) *sapIdIni* (f.p.)
saptambar (m.)	سپتمبر	September
saphI (m.)	صفہٕ	page
saphe:d (a)	سفید	white

saphar (m.)	سفر	journey
saphar na:mI (m.)	سفرنامہ	travelogue
sapha: (a)	[illegible]	clean, clear
sapha:rat kha:nI (m.)	سفارت خانہٕ	embassy
sapha: shi:n (a)	صفا شین	snow white, as white as snow
sab (f.)	سَب	row
sabIz (a)	سبزٕ	green
sabIzi: (f.)	سبزی	vegetable(s)
sabIr (m.)	صبر	patience
sabakh (m.)	سَبق	lesson/lessons
sabab (m.)	سبَب	reason
sa~ba:lun (v.m.s.)	سمبالُن	to take care, to repair *sa~ba:lIn'* (m.p.,f.s.) *sa~ba:lIni* (f.p.)
sabza:r (a)	سبزار	greenery
samIja:vun (vt.m.s.)	سمجاوُن	to make understand *samIja:vIn'* (m.p.,f.s.) *samIja:vIni* (f.p.)
samA:ji: (a)	سمآجی	social
samandar (m.)	سمنٛدر	sea, ocean
samandAri: jaha:z (m.)	سمنٛدری جہاز	ship
samandAri: pho:j (m.)	سمنٛدری فوج	navy
samay (m.)	سمَے	time
sama:ca:r (m.)	سماچار	news
sama:d (f.s.)	سماد	burial place, Samadhi *samA:z* (p)
sama:va:r (m.)	سماوار	Kashmiri tea kettle, samovar
samkhun (vi.m.s.)	سمکھُن	to meet *samkhIn'* (m.p.,f.s.) *samkhIni* (f.p.)
samtsa:r (m.)	سمژار	unity
samjun (v.m.s.)	سمجُن	to understand *samjIn'* (m.p.,f.s.) *samjIni* (f.p.)
sambal (m.)	سُمبل	crow bar
samba:lun (vt.)	سمبالُن	to repair
samsa:r (m.)	سَمسار	world
samsA:ri: (a)	سمسآری	worldly
samun (vi.)	سمَن	to meet a person, be visible
saynas (m.)	سینَس	science
saynas da:n (m.)	سینَس دان	scientist
sar (m.)	سَر	pond/ponds
sari so:bu:th (a)	سِرِ سوبوٗتھ	whole
sara:ph (m.)	صَراف	goldsmith
sara:y (m.)	سَرائے	travellers' lodge, inn
sarka:r (f.)	سرکار	government
sarkA:ri: (a)	سرکآری	official
sartal (f.)	سَرتل	brass
sarta:j (a)	سرتاج	head, great, crown, husband

sarpanc (m.)	سرپنچ	Sarpanch
saruph (m.s.)	سَرُپھ	snake *saraph* (p)
sarun (vi.)	سَرُن	to think, be careful
sarbara:h (m.)	سربراہ	leader, head
sarma:yi (m.)	سرمایہ	capital, wealth
sarsari: (a)	سرسری	ordinary, cursory
sarma:yida:r (m.)	سرمایہ دار	wealthy, captalist
salA:m' (m.)	سلامؠ	salute
salay (f.s.)	سلے	knitting needle *salyi* (p)
sala:d (f.s.)	سلاد	salad
sala:h (m.)	صلح	friendship, truce
sala:hka:r (m.)	صلحکار	advisor
saltanat (m.)	سلطنت	kingdom
sala:m (m.)	سلام	greetings
sava:l (m.)	سوال	question
saha:r (m.)	سہار	pre-dawn
sehrI (m.)	سیہرٕ	groom's chaplet, a face veil of bridegrooms
sa:gva:n (m.)	ساگوان	teak tree
sa:z (m.)	ساز	music
sa:zga:r (a)	سازگار	conducive, appropriate
sa:tI sa:tI (ad)	ساتٕہ ساتٕہ	at times
sa:th (m.)	ساتھ	auspicious time
sa:d (m.)	ساد	saint
sa:dI (a)	سادٕ	simple
sa:dIbeDo:l (m.s.)	سادٕ بےڈول	clumsy, simple but foolish
sa:yi (m.s.)	سایہ	shadow
sa:lur (m.s.)	سالُر	invitee, guest *sa:lIr'* (p)
sa:ph (a)	صاف	clean
sa:ph sa:ph (ad)	صاف صاف	clearly
sa:phI (m.)	صافہٕ	turban/turbans
sa:ban (f.s.)	صابن	soap
sa:yida:r (a)	سایہ دار	shadowy
sa:r (m.)	سار	gist
sa:rikuy (a)	سارِکُے	of everything
sa:run (vi.m.s.)	سارُن	to carry, feel *sa:rIn'* (m.p.,f.s.) *sa:rIni* (f.p.)
sa:l (f.s.)	سال	wife's sister *sA:j* (p)
sa:l (m.)	سال	feast
sa:vun (v.m.s.)	ساوُن	to put to sleep *sa:vIn'* (m.p.,f.s.) *sa:vIni* (f.p.)
sa:s (a)	ساس	thousand
sa:sIbAd' (a.m.)	ساسہٕ بدؠ	thousands
sikh (m.)	سِکھ	Sikh
sikI (m.)	سِکہٕ	coin
sigre:Th (m.)	سِگریٹھ	a cigarette
siTi:l (m.)	سٹیل	steel

sita:rI (m.)	سِتارٕ	planets
singa:r (m.)	سِنگار	make up
sipa:h (m.)	سِپاہ	soldier
siphar (a)	صِفر	zero
siya:h (a)	سِیاہ	black
siya:h cu:s (m.)	سِیاہ چوٗس	blotting paper
siya:sat (f.)	سِیاسَت	politics
siya:sat da:n (m.)	سِیاسَت دان	politician
sir (m.)	سِر	secret
siriph (ad)	صِرف	only
siriyi (m.)	سِرِیہ	sun
silI	سِلہٕ	tuberculosis
silIsilI (m.)	سِلسِلہٕ	connection, series
silA:y (f.s.)	سِلاے	stitching
sile:T (m.)	سِلیٹ	slate
sila:yi mishi:n (f.s.)	سِلایہ مشین	sewing machine *sila:yi mishi:nI* (p)
sivun (vt.m.s.)	سِوُن	to boil *sivIn'* (m.p.,f.s.) *sivIni* (f.p.)
sivA:y (c)	سِواے	without, except
si:kItuj' (f.)	سیٖکہٕ تُج	roasted meat
si:kh (m.)	سیٖکھ	iron bar
si:T (m.)	سیٖٹ	seat
si:Ti: (f.)	سیٖٹی	whistle
si:nI (m.)	سیٖنہٕ	chest,breast
si:ma:b (m.)	سیٖماب	mercurry
si:min' (f.)	سیٖمِنۍ	lioness
si:va: (f.s.)	سیٖوا	service
sekTre:T (m.)	سیکٹریٹ	secretariate
seki sha:T (m.)	سیکہ شاٹ	desert
sekh (f.)	سیکھ	sand
sezar (f.)	سیزر	frankness, simplicity
se~dIr (f.)	سینٛدٕر	sindu:r, vermillion
sedun (vi.)	سیدُن	be straight, be successful
sed' pA:Th' (ad)	سیدۍ پاٹھۍ	directly
sedis'od (ad)	سیدِ سیوٚد	parallel, in front
sed sa:ma:nI (m.)	سید سامانہٕ	whole thing, requirements
sehat (m.)	صِحت	health
sehat aphaza: muka:m (m.)	صِحت افزا مقام	health resort
se:ph (m.s.)	سیف	safe
se:r (m.)	سیر	a seer (weight)
se:ta:r (m.)	سیتار	sitar
senun (vi.)	سیٚنُن	be soft
su (pr.m.s.)	سُہ	he *tim* (m.p.) *s* (f.s.) *timI* (f.p.)
sukI (m.s.)	سُکہٕ	fast
suku:Tar (m.)	سُکوٗٹر	scooter
suc (m.)	سُچ	switch
sudIgu:r (m.s.)	سُدٕگوٗر	impotent, eunuch *sudIgu:r'* (p)

suda:run (v.m.s.)	سُدارُن	to improve *suda:rIn'* (m.p.,f.s.) *suda:rIni* (f.p.)
supA:r' (f.p.)	سُپأری	betal nut
subIh (m.)	صُبح	morning
subhan (ad)	صُبحن	in the morning
sumb (p.p.)	سُمب	equal
suy (a)	سُے	same
surIna:vun (vt.)	سُرِناوُن	to clean a vessel with ashes
surIna:vIna:vun (vc.m.s.)	سُرِناوِناوُن	to get utensils cleansed with ashes *surIna:vIna:vIn'* (m.p.,f.s.) *surIna:vIna:vIni* (f.p.)
sul (f.)	سُل	early (time)
suli (ad)	سُلِہ	early
suvun (v.m.s.)	سُوُن	to stitch *suvIn'* (m.p.,f.s.) *suvIni* (f.p.)
suvIna:vun (v.m.s.)	سُوِناوُن	to get stitched *suvIna:vIn'* (m.p.,f.s.) *suvIna:vIni* (f.p.)
su:Th (m.)	سوٗٹھ	suit of clothes
su:t (m.)	سوٗت	one tenth of an inch
su:d (m.)	سوٗد	interest
su:dIr' (m.)	سوٗدِری	money lender
su:r (m.)	سوٗر	ashes
su:rIdag (m.)	سوٗرِدگ	frost
su:rath (m.)	صوٗرتھ	shape

soku:n (m.)	سۄکوٗن	peace
sot (ad)	سۄت	slow
sotso:v (a)	سۄت سوو	motionless
soth (m.s.)	سۄتھ	dam
s'od (a.m.s.)	سیۄد	straight *sed'* (p) *sez* (a.f.s.) *sezI* (f.p.)
so:zun (vt.)	سوزُن	to send
so:run (vi.)	سورُن	be spent, to exhaust
s>~darma:l (f.s.)	سۄندرمال	a beautiful lady
son (a.m.s.)	سۄن	deep *sAn'* (m.p.,f.s.) *sanI* (f.p.)
sonIminImAr (f.s.)	سۄنہٕ مِنِہ مٲر	golden bird
sopun (m.)	سۄپُن	dream
sobu:th (m.)	ثبوٗتھ	proof
som (a.m.s.)	سۄم	smooth, equal *som'* (p) *som* (f.s.) *smi* (f.p.)
sombra:vun (v.m.s.)	سۄمبراوُن	to collect *sombra:vIn'* (m.p.,f.s.) *sombra:vIni* (f.p.)
soru:r (m.)	سۄروٗر	enjoyment
so~:cun (v.m.s.)	سوٗچُن	to think *so~:cin'* (m.p.,f.s.) *so~:cini* (f.p.)
so:z (m.)	سوز	music
so:zIn' Tu:p' (f.)	سوزِنۍ ٹوٗپۍ	a type of skull cap full of stitches

so:zIna:vun (vc.m.s.)	سوزناوُن	to send through someone *so:zIna:vIn'* (m.p.,f.s.) *so:zIna:vIni* (f.p.)
so~:th (m.)	سوٗنٛتھ	spring
so:da: (m.)	سودا	cargo, goods
so:n (m.s.)	سون	our *sA:n'* (m.p.,f.s.) *sa:ni* (f.p.)
so:ndar (f.s.)	سونٛدر	outlet for water
so:phI (m.)	صوفہٕ	sofa set
so:bI (m.)	صوبہٕ	state/states
so:bu:da:nI (m.)	سوبوٗدانہٕ	sago
so:r (m.)	سور	pig *su:rin'* (f.s.) *su:rini* (p)
so:run (v.m.s.)	سورُن	to exhaust *so:rIn'* (m.p.,f.s.) *so:rIni* (f.p.)
so:ruy (ad)	سورُے	whole
so:san (m.)	سوسَن	iris, a flower
s>kh (m.)	سۄکھ	happiness
s>kh d>kh (m.)	سۄکھ دۄکھ	ups and downs
s>khI vushun (a)	سۄکھہٕ وُشُن	luke warm
s>run (vi.)	سۄرُن	to remember
s>n (m.)	سۄن	gold
s>n (f.)	سۄن	co-wife
s>nur (m.)	سۄنر	goldsmith *s>onIr'* (p)
s>ndar (a)	سۄنٛدر	beautiful
s>phal (m.)	سۄپھل	success, fruitful
s>manI (a)	سۄمنہٕ	sincerely, with sincere mind
s>rkhi: (f.)	سۄرخی	redness, headline
s>rmI(m.)	سۄرمہٕ	collyrium
s>rmItul (m.s.)	سۄرمہٕ تُل	collyrium needle
s>rsha:vun (vt.)	سۄرشاوُن	to clean (hands)
s>srun (vi.)	سۄسرُن	to decay (of wood etc.)
s>:d (a)	سۄاد	one and a quarter
sTo:v (m.)	سٹوو	stove
sra:vun (m.)	سٕراوُن / شٕراوُن	Savan - name of the fourth month of Bikrami era
s>rgun (vi.))	سٔروگُن	be cheap, fall in price
s>rgra:vun (vt.)	سٔروگہٕ راوُن	make cheaper

h

hIkI (ad)	ہٕکہٕ	with force
hITImITI (ad)	ہٕٹہٕ مِٹہٕ	without any reason
hIndrun (v.m.s.)	ہٕنٛدرُن	to become cold *hindrIn'* (m.p.,f.s.) *hindrIni* (f.p.)
hIrun (v.m.s.)	ہٕرُن	to increase *hIrIn'* (m.p.,f.s.) *hIrIni* (f.p.)
hIs (m.)	ہٕس	provocation

hInun (vi.)	ہِنُن	to swell
hAki:m (m.)	حکیٖم	doctor
hAku:mat (f.)	حکوٗمت	rule
hAT (f.)	ہٕٹ	a piece of wood
hAtim (a)	ہٕتِم	hundredth
hAlvI (m.)	حلوٕ	pudding
hAl'do:d (m.)	ہٕلؠ دود	pain in hips
hAl' kA:n' (f.s.)	ہٕلؠ کانؠ	rib *hAl' ka:ni* (p)
hAsi:n (a)	حسیٖن	beautiful
hAsti: (f.)	ہٕستی	personality
hAs'vo:l (m.s.)	ہٕشؠ وول	elephant driver, mahout *hAs' vA:l'* (p)
hAhar (m.)	ہٕہر	wife's brother
hA:kim (m.)	حاکِم	ruler
hA~:kal (f.s.)	ہانٛکل	latch, bolt *hA~:kIlI* (p)
hA:j (m.)	حاج	Muslim Haj piligrimage
hA~:z (m.)	ہانٛز	boatman
hA:zim (a)	ہاضِم	digestive
hA:zir (a)	حاضِر	present
hA~:Th (a.f.s.)	ہانٛٹھ	barren, sterile *ha~:chi* (p)
hA:disI (m.)	حادِثہٕ	calamity, accident
hA:bath (m.)	ہابتھ	terror
hA:r (f.s.)	ہار	maina - starling *ha:ri* (p)

hA:rA:ni: (f.)	حآرآنی	astonishment, surprise
hA:sil (m.)	حاصِل	achievement,
hAki:kath (m.)	حقیٖقتھ	truth, reality
hakrun (vi.)	ہکرُن	be hard
hakhur (m.s.)	ہکھُر	young bull *hakhar* (p)
hatsarlad (a)	ہٕژرلد	helpless, grief stricken
haTh (m.)	ہٹھ	blister
hatIbAd' (a.m.p.)	ہتہٕ بدؠ	hundreds of
hatIzangul (m.)	ہتہٕ زنٛگل	centipede *hatIzangal* (p)
hatab (m.)	ہتب	fire wood
hath (a)	ہتھ	hundred
had (m.)	حد	limit
hadI nebar (ad)	حدٕ نیبر	beyond limit
hana: (ad)	ہنا	a little
hangI tI mangI (ad)	ہنگہٕ تہٕ منگہٕ	suddenly
hand (n)	ہنٛد	dandelion, a green vegetable
haphtI (m.)	ہفتہٕ	a week
habush (m.s.)	حبُش	wild, African *habIsh* (p)
hame:shI (ad)	ہمیشہٕ	always
hama:l (m.)	ہمال	porter
hamla:var (m.)	حملاوَر	invader
hamun (v)	ہمُن	to be mild

hamdardi: (f.)	ہمدردی	sympathy
hamso:s (m.)	ہمسوس	desire, woe, remorse
hamlI (m.)	حملہٕ	attack
hamlI karun (cv.)	حملہٕ کرُن	to attack
haya:h (m.)	حیاہ	modesty, shyness
harIj (m.)	حٕرج	obstacle, disturb
harIj karun	حٕرج کرُن	to disturb, to put obstacles
harga:h (c)	ہرگاہ	if
hargiz (ad)	ہرگِز	ever, not on any account
harja:nI (m.)	ہرجانہٕ	penalty
harta:l (m.)	ہرتال	strike
harud (m.)	ہرُد	autumn
harshA:mIts (a.f.s.)	ہرشآمٕژ	married woman *harsha:yimatsI* (p)
harun (vi.)	ہرُن	to drip
hal (m.)	حَل	solution
halam (m.s.)	ہلم	lap
halkI (m.)	ہلکہٕ	area, light (weight)
halkIda:r (m.)	ہلکہٕ دار	patwari - a revenue official
halph (m.)	حلف	cath
hale:lI (m.)	ہلیلہٕ	myrobalam
halvo:y (m.s.)	حلوٕے	confectioner *halvA:y* (p)
havA:yi: aDI (m.)	ہوٲئی اڈٕ	airport
havA:yi pho:j (m.)	ہوٲئی فوج	air force
havan (m.)	ہوَن	Yajna
havas (m.)	ہوَس	desire, lust
hava: (m.)	ہوا	wind
hava:lI (m.)	حوالہٕ	description, entrusted with
hava:la:Th (m.)	حوالاٹھ	prison
hava:lda:r (m.)	حوالدار	head constable
hash (f.s.)	ہَش	mother-in-law *hashI* (p)
hasad (m.)	حسد	jealousy
hasar (m.)	حسَر	importance
haspata:l (m.)	ہسپتال	hospital
hasrat (f.)	حسرت	longing, wonder
ha:ki: (f.)	ہاکی	hockey
ha:kh (m.)	ہاکھ	sweede, khol-khol
ha~:gul (m.)	ہانٛگُل	deer
ha~:tsh (f.s.)	ہانٛژھ	allegation
ha:jath (m.)	حاجتھ	need
ha:nIDu:n (m.s.)	ہانٛزٕ ڈوٗن	chesnut, wild nut, aesculus indica
ha:pIts (f.s.)	ہاپٕژ	she bear *ha:pItsI* (p)
ha:put (m.s.)	ہاپُت	he bear *ha:path* (p)
ha:m (f.s.)	ہام	a kind of weed, penicum colonum *ha:mI* (p)

ha:y (i)	ہاے	oh!
ha:r (m.)	ہار	necklace
ha:r (f.)	ہار	defeat
ha:rI (m.)	ہارٕ	money
ha:run (vi.)	ہارُن	surrender, be defeated
ha:run (v.m.s.)	ہارُن	to lose *ha:rIn'* (m.p.,f.s.) *ha:rIni* (f.p.)
ha:l (ad)	حال	present, detail
ha:lath (f.)	حالَتھ	condition
ha:lav (m.)	ہالَو	locust
ha:las (ad)	حالَس	for the time being
ha:vun (v.m.s.)	ہاوُن	to show *ha:vIn'* (m.p.,f.s.) *ha:vIni* (f.p.)
h'a:vun (vc.m.s.)	ہیاوُن	to make someone buy *h'a:vIn'* (m.p.,f.s.) *h'a:vIni* (f.p.)
hikIT (f.s.)	ہِکٕٹ	dance performed by two women *hikIci* (p)
hickica:haTh (f.)	ہِچکِچاہَٹھ	hesitation
hith (m.)	ہِتھ	excuse
hira:s (m.)	ہِراس	precaution
hir'gogul (m.)	ہِرِ گوگُل	vocal cord
hir'vo:l (m.)	ہِرِ وول	oesephagus
hilun (v)	ہِلُن	to move
hishar (m.)	ہِشَر	relation, similarity
hisI (m.)	حِصٕہ	part
hisIkAshi: (f.)	حِصہٕ کٔشی	division
hisa:b (m.)	حِساب	arithmetic, account
hi:Tar (m.)	ہیٖٹَر	heater
hi: thAr (f.s.)	ہی ٹھٔر	jasmine, a flower plant *hi:thari* (p)
hi:r (f.s.)	ہیٖر	head, skull *he:ri* (p)
hi:ro: (m.)	ہیٖرو	hero
hi:ro:yin (f.)	ہیٖرویِن	heroine
hi:lIbaha:nI (m.)	ہیٖلہٕ بہانہٕ	excuses
hekath (f.s.)	ہیٚکَتھ	strength
hekun (v.m.s.)	ہیٚکُن	to be able *hekIn'* (m.p.,f.s.) *hekIni* (f.p.)
hechun (v.m.s.)	ہیٚچھُن	to learn *hechIn'* (m.p.,f.s.) *hechIni* (f.p.)
hechIna:vun (v.m.s.)	ہیٚچھناوُن	to teach *hechIna:vIn'* (m.p.,f.s.) *hechIna:vIni* (f.p.)
heDun (m.s.)	ہیٚڈُن	mock, to criticise, reproach *heDIn'* (m.p.,f.s.) *heDIni* (f.p.)
heDur (m.s.)	ہیٚڈُر	mushroom *heDar* (p)
hekun (vi.)	ہیٚکُن	be able to undertake or lift
heng (m.)	ہیٚنٛگ	horn/horns

hendIvend (m.)	ہینٛدِوینٛد	water-melon
hendusta:n (m.)	ہندوستان	India
hapha:zat (m.)	حفاظت	defence, protection
hemI (m.)	ہیٚمہ	beans
hemath (f.)	ہِمتھ	courage
he:r (f.s.)	ہیر	stair case *he:rI* (p)
herI b>nI (ad)	ہیرِ بوٚنہٕ	up and down
hesI (ad)	ہیسہ	carefully
he: (i)	ہے	oh !
he:ji (m.p.)	ہیجے	spellings
he:rath (f.s.)	ہیرتھ	Shivaratri
h'uk (m.s.)	ہیُک	hiccup *hik'* (p)
hu (pr.m.s.)	ہُہ	he, that one hum (m.p.)
h> (f.s.)	ہوٚ	she *humI* (f.p.)
hukumra:n (m.)	حُکمران	ruler(s)
hutinas (ad)	ہُتِنٕس	there
hut'a th (ad)	ہُتیتھ	there (locational)
hudun (v.m.s.)	ہُدُن	to dig
hu~dur (ad)	ہُنٛدُر	cold
hupA:r' (ad)	ہُپارؠ	in that direction
humun (vi)	ہُمُن	sacrificial oblation
hom'sund (p.pr.m.s.)	ہوٚمیٚسُنٛد	his *hom' sInd'* (p)

hom'sInz (f.s.)	ہوٚمیٚسٕنٛز	her *hom' sInzI* (p)
homra:vun (vt.)	ہوٚمراوُن	to pacify
huy (m.s.)	ہُے	noise
hur (a)	ہُر	extra
hure:ma:nI (a)	ہُریمانہٕ	extra
h'vuy (a.m.s.)	ہیُوٗے	similar *hiviy* (m.p.) *hishiy* (f.s.) *hishay* (f.p.)
hushya:r (a)	ہُشیار	active, wakeful
husun (m.)	حُسُن	beauty
huhund (p.pr.m.s.)	ہُہُنٛد	their, their's *huhInd'* (m.p.) *huhInz* (f.s.) *huhInzi* (f.p.)
hu:n (m.s.)	ہوٗن	dog *hu:n'* (p)
hu:n' (f.s.)	ہوٗنؠ	bitch *ho:ni* (f.p.)
hu:bahu: (a)	ہوٗبہوٗ	similar, exactly resembling
hu:r (f.s.)	حوٗر	fairy, hourie *hu:rI* (p)
hu:rI vanvun (m)	حوٗرِ وَنوُن	celecial song/music
hokum (m.)	حوٚکُم	order
hokh (a)	ہوٚکھ	dry
h>khIr (f.s.)	ہوٚکھٕر	young female calf *hokhIri* (p)
hokhIs'un (m.)	ہوٚکھٕ سیُن	dry vegetable

h>khIna:vun (v.m.s.)	ہۆکھناوُن	to dry *hkhIna:vIn'* (m.p.,f.s.) *hkhIna:vIni* (f.p.)
h>ga:DI (f.)	ہۆگاڑ	dried fish
hots (m.s.)	ہۆژ	wrist *hAts'* (p)
hoT (f.s.)	ہۆٹ	throat *hAT'* (p)
hot (ad)	ہۆت	there (directional)
hotImut (a.m.s.)	ہۆتہٕمُت	rotten *hAt' mIt'* (p) *hotsmIts* (f.s.) *hotsImatsI* (f.p.)
hoti (ad)	ہوتہٕ	there (locational)
hota:m (ad)	ہوتام	upto that point
h'ot d'ot (m.)	ہیۆت دیۆت	dowry
h'on (v.m.s.)	ہیۆن	to buy, to start, to feel (pain for someone) *hen'* (m.p.,f.s.) *heni* (f.p.)
h'ondustA:n' (m.)	ہیٚنٛدُستٲنؠ	Indian
h'or (ad)	ہیۆر	up
hol (a.m.s.)	ہۆل	twisted, bent *hAl'* (p) *hAj* (f.s.) *haji* (f.p.)
hol tI kol	ہۆل تہٕ کۆل	curved, not straight, crooked
h'ol (m.s.)	ہیۆل	ear of corn, twig *hel'* (p)
hos (m.s.)	ہۆس	elephant *hAs'* (p)
h'ohar (m.s.)	ہیۆہر	father-in-law *h' ehar* (p)
ho:Tal (m.)	ہوٹل	hotel
ho:g (f.s.)	ہوگ	rumour
ho:z (m.s.)	حوض	pond
ho:nIha:r (a)	ہونہٕہار	intelligent
ho:r (ad)	ہور	there (directional)
ho:run (v.m.s.)	ہورُن	to clear up, to pay *ho:rIn'* (m.p.,f.s.) *ho:rIni* (f.p.)
ho:r kun (ad)	ہورکُن	in that direction
ho:lDar (m.)	ہولڈر	pen
ho:lDa:l (m.)	ہول ڈال	hold-all
ho:slI (m.)	حوصلہٕ	courage, good manners
ho:sh (a)	ہوش	awareness, sense
h>~gan' (f.s.)	ہۆنٛگنؠ	chin *h>~ngIni* (p)
h>char (m.s.)	ہۆچھر	dryness
h>khun (vi.)	ہۆکھُن	become dry, to dry up
h>khIna:vun (vt.)	ہۆکھناوُن	make dry
h>tsun (v.m.s.)	ہۆژُن	to rot, decay, decompose *h>tsIn'* (m.p.,f.s.) *h>tsIni* (f.p.)
h>tsIra:vun (vt.)	ہۆژراوُن	cause to rot
h>lIhAj (f.)	ہۆلہٕہٲج	measles